FINDING HAY

A JOURNEY UP BROAD STREET

FINDING HAY

A JOURNEY UP BROAD STREET

Rosie Hayles

LOGASTON PRESS

FRONT COVER: View along Broad Street, c.1900 (photo courtesy of Eric Pugh).

BACK COVER: Drawing, dated 1879, by J.C. Haddon, Architects, of proposed changes to the Rose and Crown (Photo courtesy of William Beales & Co.)

FRONTISPIECE: Detail from *Hay on Wye and the Brecon Beacons*, 1846, by Joseph Murray Ince, 1806–59 (image courtesy of The National Library of Wales).

First published in 2022 by Logaston Press
The Holme, Church Road, Eardisley HR3 6NJ, UK
www.logastonpress.co.uk
An imprint of Fircone Books Ltd.

ISBN 978-1-910839-58-4

Text copyright © Rosie Hayles, 2022.
All black and white photographs copyright © Eric Pugh (with thanks to contributors to his work) unless otherwise stated below the image.
All colour photographs copyright © Darren Elliott or Richard Wheeler unless otherwise stated below the image.
All plans courtesy of Lawrie Cartwright unless otherwise stated below the image.

All rights reserved.
The moral right of the author has been asserted.

Without limiting the rights under copyright reserved above, no part of this publication may be reproduced, stored in or introduced into a retrieval system, or transmitted, in any form or by any means (electronic, mechanical, photocopying, recording or otherwise), without prior written permission of the copyright owner and the above publisher of this book.

Designed and typeset by Richard Wheeler in 11 on 15 Garamond.
Cover design by Richard Wheeler.

Printed and bound in the UK.

Logaston Press is committed to a sustainable future for our business, our readers and our planet. This book is made from paper certified by the Forest Stewardship Council.

British Library Catalogue in Publishing Data.
A CIP catalogue record for this book is available from the British Library.

CONTENTS

	PREFACE	vii
	ACKNOWLEDGEMENTS AND DEDICATION	ix
1	The Normans	1
2	The Town Wall, the Burgage Holders and a Visiting Antiquary	23
3	Broad Street Houses, a Jacobean Mansion and the First Bridge	39
4	Two Railways, The Crown and the Clock Tower	57
5	The Café Royal and the First World War	89
6	The Armstrong Case	107
7	A Petrol Pump on the Pavement and the Second World War	117
8	Rampaging Cows and a Fourth Bridge	143
9	Richard Booth Creates a Booktown	159
	AFTERWORD	179
	ENDNOTES	181
	BIBLIOGRAPHY	187
	INDEX	191

A simplified plan of Broad Street today, with previous names and uses italicised in brackets

PREFACE

Why Broad Street? It's a question several people have asked.

Broad Street is a short road that runs along the lower edge of Hay, so it can be surprising to learn that it was at the very heart of town life from Norman times right through to the early part of the twentieth century.

The Hay Mills were here, and for centuries it was Broad Street that provided town and castle with bread, ale, meat, leather and other essentials of medieval life. The cattle market was held here until 1919, with all the attendant market stalls, pubs, café, grocers, tailor, doctor and solicitors required by farmers and their wives. The Seven Stars used to be twice its present length and an important coaching inn. And the main open-air meeting place for the town was at the end of the road by the clock tower.

On a personal level, my long fascination with the history of Hay, and Broad Street in particular, began when I went to live there with my daughter in 1986. Two years later we bought West House and I became intrigued by the complex relationship between it and No. 22, the house next door. From the front they look completely different. One is short and broad; the other tall and thin. Yet their back rooms had apparently once been part of the same malthouse. Even today they are separated only by a thin partition and share a single window on the ground floor.

Conveyancing for the purchase of West House in 1988 was done by Martin Beales, the solicitor across the road. Sadly, he would die in 2010. Yet in my mind's eye I can still see him sitting at his desk with a huge legal tome in front of him, mystified by my attempts to explain how one of the West House bedrooms could be above one of those in No. 22. 'Must be a flying freehold' he concluded eventually. He would go on to write an award-winning book about Herbert Rowse Armstrong, the alleged poisoner, who had once sat at that same desk. The copy he signed for me would provide a stimulating introduction to the famous case.

The Granary, by the clock tower at the other end of the road, would become something of a home from home with its open fire. I would go there for coffee every morning and Anna Golesworthy would join me occasionally.

And so I began to collect and be fascinated by stories of those who had lived or worked on Broad Street. Many came simply from talking to people, others from written material, published and unpublished. At the same time, however, the town's Norman beginnings were throwing up some intriguing questions. Why was St Mary's Church so far from the centre of town? Why were there two Norman castles within a few yards of each other? And what of that strange name The Hay?

Then there were the accounts of those who had visited the town and walked along Broad Street in Tudor, Stuart and Victorian times. I began to see how Broad Street could provide the focus for a new look at the history of Hay itself and, on impulse, rang Richard Wheeler at Logaston Press. 'How would you like to consider a book …?' And so began the serious work, and the great pleasure, of researching further and writing it all up.

The Covid-19 lock-downs provided the leisure to bring it all to completion.

NB *The word 'now', scattered throughout, refers to the winter of 2021/ 2022.*

Rosie Hayles, 2022

ACKNOWLEDGEMENTS

The author wishes to express her grateful thanks to all those who have contributed to the making of this book, and they are many. The main contributors are named in the text but the ideas, memories and support of those not named have been much valued nonetheless.

To publishers Richard and Su Wheeler also, much gratitude for the friendly patience and skill with which they have dealt with an inexperienced author.

DEDICATION

This book is dedicated to all who have known and loved Hay, past and present, and in particular to the memory of those who have, sadly, passed away since making their contribution to the writing of it:

Albert Powell
Tony Pugh
Pat Thornton
Peter and Eileen Underhill

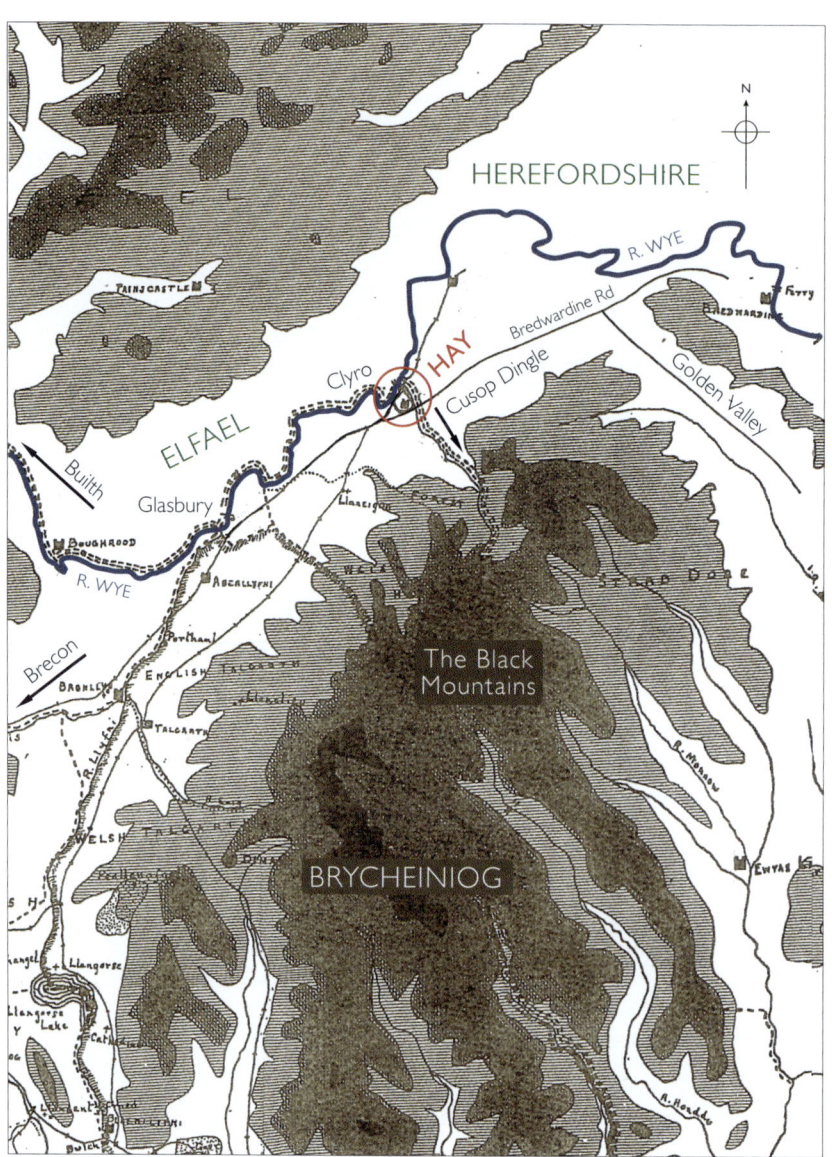

Map of the landscape setting of Hay, based on a map by William Rees in 'The Medieval Lordship of Brecon' (*The Transactions of the Honourable Society of Cymmrodorion*, 1915)

The Normans

Until the Normans came storming across the Welsh border in the eleventh century there appears to have been no settlement at Hay of any kind.[1] There was only a wooded hill whose northern flank dropped steeply to the River Wye. Welsh farmland stretched away towards the Black Mountains in the south and west, while a brook called the Dulais wound around the base of this hill to the east.

The Dulais brook was crossed by a country lane, part of which would eventually be levelled and widened so that markets could be held there. This would become Broad Street. The houses along its northern side would look up to a castle across an open expanse of hillside on which animals grazed, for it would be the first road to be occupied in a new town the Normans would call La Haye.

The hill was in the ancient Welsh kingdom of Brycheiniog, but only just. Across the Dulais Brook was Herefordshire and England,[2] while on the other side of the Wye the Welsh land of Elfael stretched almost to Builth. It was therefore at the extreme tip of three distinct territories. Border country with a vengeance.

William FitzOsbern

The first incursion of the Normans into Brycheiniog made little impact on the hill. The earl of Hereford was a high-ranking baron of incorrigibly martial disposition called William FitzOsbern, who did invade Welsh territory at this point, but soon departed, yielding to the call of greater gains to be had elsewhere.

He was one of the privileged band of Norman barons known as Marcher lords, from the Old English word 'mearc', meaning boundary. The territory they governed was known as the Welsh Marches and at those times when they felt they had the freedom to invade Wales at will it expanded rapidly. William FitzOsbern had secured a foothold in Wales by laying the foundations of a huge castle at Chepstow within a year of the Conquest. But it was from his more basic motte and bailey[3] at Clifford, two miles downstream from the Dulais Brook, that he took an army over the border formed by this brook and into Brycheiniog in the summer of 1070.

◆◆◆

NORMAN CASTLES

The Normans introduced both castles of stone and the more primitive motte and baileys to Britain, driving them like nails into conquered landscapes to hold Norman sovereignty in place.

Their huge stone castles were built in prominent positions as monuments to the intended permanence of Norman domination; constant and humiliating reminders to the Welsh and English that they were conquered peoples. Wales in particular had to endure the presence of an inordinate number and has been described as the medieval castle capital of the world.

Motte and bailey castles were simple to construct and sprang up rapidly all across the land. The motte was an earthen mound surrounded by a ditch and topped by a wooden tower, which acted as both emergency refuge and lookout post. The bailey was a protected flat area adjacent to the motte that was used to house the barracks, stables, kitchens, smithies and other ancillary buildings. The countryside around Hay is still littered with large grassy mounds that have no modern purpose but once formed the mottes of these early castles.

◆◆◆

A few yards from the Dulais Brook, FitzOsbern's army crossed the point where, in future years, a gate would bar entry to the town of La Haye. Ahead lay a short, steep hill, and beyond that the more level section that would become Broad Street. But they could know nothing of that. To them it was just a country lane taking them across the northern flank of a hill. Half a mile from the Dulais they encountered the steep ravine of the Login Brook, but there was nothing to tell them that a Norman church would one day stand close by. They simply marched on, penetrating ever deeper into Brycheiniog where they would eventually defeat three Welsh princes.

William FitzOsbern might well have gone on to establish his hold on this part of mid Wales if he hadn't been distracted at that point by a proposal of marriage. His first wife had died and he was now approached by the recently widowed countess of Flanders, Richilde, who wanted his help in defending the duchy against her brother-in-law. It presented FitzOsbern with a dilemma. If he married Richilde he would be count of Flanders but it would mean leaving Wales immediately and jeopardising the possible future success of his campaign there. Flanders was the greater prize, however, so he withdrew his army from Brycheiniog and took it across the Channel, where he is assumed to have married Richilde shortly before being killed in battle there on 22 February 1071. Her brother-in-law was left to claim the victory.

La Haye
Norman attempts to conquer Brycheiniog ceased for some time after that but the name 'Hay' suggests that knights from Clifford castle continued to cross the Dulais in order to hunt. The French name for Hay was La Haye, a term usually translated as an enclosure, a hedged enclosure, or simply a hedge. But in Norman times it seems to have indicated an enclosure in which deer were kept prior to a hunt.

Hunting played a significant role in the lives of Norman knights, as it had for the Roman cavalry, contributing an important cross-country element to the long and arduous training needed for fighting from horseback. But time spent locating deer was time wasted, so stalkers on foot were sent out in advance to find prime specimens and entice them into a haye. There they could be kept until a hunt was due; but then, when a horn gave the signal, they were released and the chase was on.[4] In medieval times a hunt was often referred to simply as 'the chase'.

Domesday Book does not usually include Welsh territory and Hay is not mentioned, but there are numerous references to hayes in Herefordshire. They are often in woods and usually associated with land that is 'waste', or not currently in use as farmland. The entry for Titley, between Kington and Presteigne, is typical:

> There is land for 6 ploughs. It was, and is, waste. However, there is there 1 haye [hedged enclosure] in a little wood.[5]

If there was indeed a haye between the Dulais and the Login then it may well have covered all that part not crossed by country lanes, thus giving the name La Haye to the whole hill. Alternatively it might have been somewhat smaller and on the site of either the castle – or, more likely, the present cattle market.

Bernard de Neufmarché

William FitzOsbern had been loyal to William the Conqueror but the son who succeeded him as earl of Hereford, was not. Known as Roger de Breteuil (from the family holding of Breteuil in Normandy) he took part in a rebellion that became known as the Revolt of the Earls and it proved his undoing. In 1075 he was deprived of all his lands and titles, and after spending almost all the rest of his life in prison, he was eventually beheaded. He had been earl of Hereford for just four years.

The Revolt of the Earls was a wake-up call for William the Conqueror. It brought home to him just how dangerously powerful the Marcher lords were becoming and he allowed no further forays into south Wales during his lifetime. He may even have made a pact with the powerful Welsh prince Rhys ap Tewdwr to that effect.[6]

When his son, William Rufus, came to the throne in 1087, however, that policy appears to have changed. Rufus too faced rebellion but chose the path of appeasement and seems to have given at least tacit consent to the launch of further attacks on south Wales. The position was unclear enough for an obscure knight called Bernard de Neufmarché, or Bernard Newmarch, to take the risk of assembling an army and setting out for Brycheiniog.

According to Domesday Book, and in marked contrast to William

FitzOsbern, Bernard de Neufmarché held no English lands at all in 1086, although he also had been with the Conqueror at Hastings. Shortly after 1086, however, he was granted lands in the Golden Valley, including the castles of Urishay, Snodhill and Dorstone, and from that direction he could enter Brycheiniog via the Bredwardine road.

William FitzOsbern's route had taken him across the northern side of the hill that would become Hay. But Bernard de Neufmarché marched his army across its southern flank, close by the summit, and it may have occurred to him then that the hilltop would make an ideal site for a castle. Indeed, it might already have been encircled by the hedged perimeter of a haye. But he marched his army on, and took Glasbury before the end of 1088.

It would be another five years before the whole of Brycheiniog came under his control, but in 1093 he managed to defeat its king at the Battle of Brecon, and that king's overlord, Rhys ap Tewdwr, was killed soon afterwards. The new Marcher lordship of Brecon was created from the tattered remains of Brycheiniog and finally, in his mid-forties, Bernard de Neufmarché found himself acknowledged as a Marcher lord. He could now rule with almost regal powers over his English and Welsh vassals.

There are no written records of Hay from this period, but it seems from the archaeology that a castle was built on the hilltop at about this time. The partially ruined square keep that can be seen today was part of it, although when first built it had a gateway through the middle.[7]

Interestingly, however, there was a motte and bailey in the close vicinity that appears to have come into existence at more or less the same time. The motte is still visible near the church, and the bailey presumably extended over the present cattle market site. But why two castles so close together? The one on the hilltop was built in stone and if that came first there would have been no need for the motte and bailey. But the motte and bailey cannot have come first because it would have been subject to attack from the nearby hilltop. So what was going on?

One possible answer is that the motte and bailey was in fact a former haye; a large, ready-hedged enclosure called into use as a secure base for men and materials during the initial phases of constructing the masonry castle on the hilltop. The motte, by this token, would have been thrown up to give extra height to the sentry on look-out duty in exactly the same way as it would in a fully-formed motte and bailey castle. There are no signs of a tower having been erected on the top of the one in Hay.

A craze was spreading across northern Europe at that time for castles to incorporate a small market town within their precincts, and Hay too would follow that pattern. The town was enclosed within what was, in effect, the outer bailey of the hilltop castle, with the motte and bailey abutting it to the west.

The route through this new Norman castle-town was a gated section of the country lane once taken by FitzOsbern and his army as they marched across the hill from Clifford. But it was a section divided, by name and gradient, into three parts.

The central, levelled part would become Broad Street, the first road to be occupied. This was where markets would be held and where the town's corn mill would be situated. At the eastern end of Broad Street the lane dropped to the Dulais Brook, a pitch now called Newport Street, while at the western end it continued uphill for the short distance that has become Belmont Road.

Houses were built only on the outer side of Broad Street so that their occupants, and the markets, could be kept under constant surveillance from the castle. The occupants were English, the farmers attending the markets mostly Welsh, and both were now subject to tight Norman control.

The motte of Hay's motte and bailey castle c.1880 with toll gate and keeper

An engraving (by J. Hinchcliffe after Henry Gastineau) of Hay Church as it was c.1830, shortly before it was demolished and rebuilt as now. (Image courtesy of antiqueprints.com)

The centre of the town remained largely open hillside with animals grazing there – food on the hoof in case of need. For La Haye was an isolated settlement and always at risk of attack.

For the first inhabitants of La Haye, living on Broad Street, it must have come as a surprise to find that they had to leave the town and walk almost half a mile to hear Mass on a Sunday. Why, they must have wondered, had the Normans built the church outside the protection of both castles? It was near the motte, but on the far side of a deep cleft in the land carved out by the Login Brook. They had to cross the Login to get to it. Why?

Nothing now remains of the church attended by those early settlers of Broad Street, but it is assumed to have been on the same site as the present one, and the reason for this particular choice of location remains something of a mystery. In other places the Normans built a church to replace a Welsh 'clas' (or 'glas' as in Glasbury) but not, apparently, at Hay. Here, it seems more likely that the site held some other kind of special significance for the Welsh, which the Normans wanted to overlay with their own, strictly hierarchical, brand of Christianity.

Celtic Christianity (so-called) had been practised in Wales for hundreds of years before the Normans arrived, but in country areas the pagan beliefs of the early Celts still maintained some residual association with certain places. Healing wells, waterfalls and the confluence of watercourses often continued to be held sacred.

St Mary's Church is exceptionally well placed in relation to all of these. It is on a knoll from which the land drops steeply into the deep dingle cut by the Login Brook to the east. The Login tumbles over a waterfall at this point before flowing out into the Wye, and near the confluence are two freshwater springs, known as the Eye Well and the Walk Well. Then, St Mary's Well is immediately to the west and the Swan Well to the south. There can hardly have been a site more conducive to the worship, or at least the honouring, of flowing water.[8]

The Welsh name for Hay is Y Gelli Gandryll, the shattered grove. Some have said that this was the Welsh version of the Norman 'La Haye', and some that it was the other way round, but neither is particularly convincing. A grove is not the same thing as a hedged enclosure. It seems more likely that Y Gelli Gandryll was the name given by the Welsh to a place where

LEFT TO RIGHT: The confluence of the Login Brook and River Wye; the Login waterfall from below; the Swan Well flows into the Login Brook behind the Swan Hotel

an important grove of trees had been destroyed, and it takes only a small stretch of the imagination to see such a grove on the knoll now occupied by Hay Church.

Sometime between 1115 and 1121 Bernard de Neufmarché attended a ceremony to dedicate the new Norman church on this site to 'the blessed Mary'. And as the Bishop of St David's sermonised, he perhaps allowed his mind to wander. He had conquered the whole of Brycheiniog in the 30 years since his army had marched past the place where he was now standing. Its ancient capital had been demolished and the new town of Brecon was growing up around the castle he had built there.

Here at La Haye a small market town had been established within the precincts of the castle and he no doubt reflected on the arrangement with some satisfaction. It gave maximum control over the townspeople at the same time as it facilitated additional taxation of the local farmers.

The Welsh farmers, whose lands stretched from Hay towards the Black Mountains, had been allowed to retain their farms in return for the payment of rent. But the money for that rent had to come from the sale of whatever they could sell at market, so de Neufmarché gained at every point. He could charge for entry into his gated market town and then tax every transaction conducted within it. The cattle market on Broad Street would have been especially lucrative in that respect, for black Welsh cattle were in high demand. Anyone who forestalled by trading outside the market place could be fined. The corn mill on Broad Street was his and he could charge for the compulsory use of it, as also for the brewery and bakehouse on that same site. In fact, from his point of view it was an altogether inspired arrangement.

Not that he dealt with any of these matters personally. He had a bailiff, a constable in charge of the castle, and a number of townspeople on the manorial court, which met at the castle and collected rents and tolls on his behalf.

Most of the townspeople had been drafted in, willingly or otherwise, from his estates in Herefordshire. His steward had selected those he thought most suitable to become the new town's millers, butchers, tanners, brewers, slaughtermen and other essential tradesmen – and they hadn't done badly out of it, Bernard no doubt reflected. Each had come with his family, if he had one, and been allowed a burgage plot with a house on it. The burgage holder became a burgess, eligible to take part in the governance of the town, and the plots were large enough for each family to be at least partially self-sufficient. He had given the burgesses the right to hand down burgage tenancies from one generation to the next, so it was now in their own interest to guard his town and castle against any retaliation by the dispossessed Welsh. Clever.

But if Bernard's reflections on the town gave him some satisfaction, he probably avoided thinking about his wife. He had followed the usual Marcher pattern of conquering through force and then opting for permanent settlement through marriage into the Welsh nobility, and it had brought him heartache.

His wife was called Nest, or Agnest, and she must have been about 14 to his late-30s when they married in 1088, soon after he had taken Glasbury. There was also considerable disparity between them in social standing. Agnest was the daughter of Nest, the famously beautiful and resourceful daughter of Gruffydd ap Llewelyn – considered to be the first and last King of Wales – and Ealdgyth, daughter of the earl of Mercia. For her second husband Ealdgyth had married Harold Godwinson, King of England before the Norman Conquest. At the time of their marriage, then, Agnest had been the daughter of two royal houses, while her husband's origins had been relatively obscure.

Agnest had a nephew, known to us as Gerald of Wales, and although she was his aunt he tells the following story about her.[9] Agnest, he says, fell in love with a knight who was not her husband, and her son, a youth called Mahel, took exception to the liaison. He beat the knight and mutilated him, whereupon Agnest became determined to have him disinherited. So she went to the king and swore on oath that Mahel was not Bernard's son but the child of another man. In this, says Gerald of Wales, she was perjuring herself, though he does not explain how he could possibly have acquired this intimate knowledge. For him it was 'not to be wondered at if a woman bears malice, for this comes to her naturally'. Gerald was Archdeacon of Brecon and well steeped in the Church's attitude towards women.

It suited Henry I, however, to believe Agnest, for Brecon was in a key, strategic location. If Mahel were disinherited, then Agnest's daughter, Sybil, would become heir to its lordship and he could marry Sybil to his most loyal subject, a man called Miles of Gloucester. The pair would then form a bulwark for him against the growing power of the southern Marcher lords.

The marriage of Sybil de Neufmarché to Miles of Gloucester took place in 1121, and for her dowry Henry 1 granted almost everything her father owned to Miles, with right of succession to the remainder on his death. Bernard de Neufmarché must have been about 70 by that time and may have been ill. He and Agnest had already lost a son called Philip and perhaps the shock of finding that Mahel was not his son had been more than he could take. He would die sometime between 1123 and 1125.

Life in the Early Town

The first people to move into La Haye would have come from Bernard de Neufmarché's estates in rural Herefordshire, and it no doubt took them some considerable time to adjust to life in a town. Towns and villages were few and far between in Anglo-Saxon England, as in Wales. Most people lived on family farmsteads. After 1066, however, the Normans began herding people into villages to keep them under close control, and in towns like Hay that control was taken a stage further still. Here, they were not only forced to live on standardised plots closely lined up along a street, they were confined within the precincts of a Norman castle isolated in Welsh countryside.

And somehow or other they had to earn money. They had to pay rent on their burgages, plus an annual burgage fee. They were charged for the compulsory use of their lord's brewhouse and bakehouse and, if they had corn from an agricultural strip outside the town, his mill. They were even charged for the right to fish the Wye.

The first plots were almost certainly on Broad Street, created from the level part of the now enclosed section of country lane running from Clifford to Glasbury. On the outer side of the road only, the plots were narrow (road frontage being at a premium) but they stretched a long way back. From the far end their occupants could have looked down on the River Wye 100 feet and more below if there hadn't been a fence, or perhaps a hedge, to protect them from the Welsh. For this was the town boundary. The town wall would not be built for another 200 years.

Each plot had a house that opened straight onto the street, and behind it were sheds and workshops with, often, a pigsty. The practice of hanging the carcass of a slaughtered pig from the door of a garden shed would continue in the town until well into the 1940s. Most households kept chickens and the entire population would have been woken each day by crowing cockerels. Beyond the outbuildings were sections for vegetables, fruit trees and the herbs needed for cooking, flavouring ale and medicines.

All Hay's medieval houses are long gone, but Powys House at 15 Broad Street stands on one of the few burgage plots in the town that remain in more or less their original state. The Norman passion for control kept them all to standard sizes measured in units called perches, a perch being equal to approximately 16½ feet (5 m). The Powys House plot is two perches wide and 17 perches from the street to the top of the riverbank. The house doubles as a shop and an alleyway beside it offers entry to the plot beyond. It is an arrangement that would have been much the same in Norman times.

◆◆◆

THE MILL SITE

The lord's mill at Hay was on Broad Street, high above the Wye. Its site was a large one at the top of the Newport Street pitch, and contained at various times at least two mill wheels running off a mill pond, plus a brewery and a tannery. Much of the complex would remain in use until the early part of the twentieth century.

By making the use of flour mill and brewery compulsory, the lord gained a monopoly on the production of both bread and ale, those two staples of the medieval diet. Flour was also used to make the deep pastry cases filled with pulverised meat and herbs that were as handy for taking to work as the Cornish pasty. Ale was drunk by all medieval commoners, even children drinking small ale with 1–1½% alcohol. The only thing that differentiated ale from today's beer was the flavouring. Hyssop and burdock root were popular, or perhaps marigold. Hops did not come in from the Netherlands until the 1400s.

There was no need for a flour mill to be situated close to the Wye, and having it there had involved digging out a millstream right across town. So it seems that the mill site was designed from the outset to include a tannery. The noxious fluids

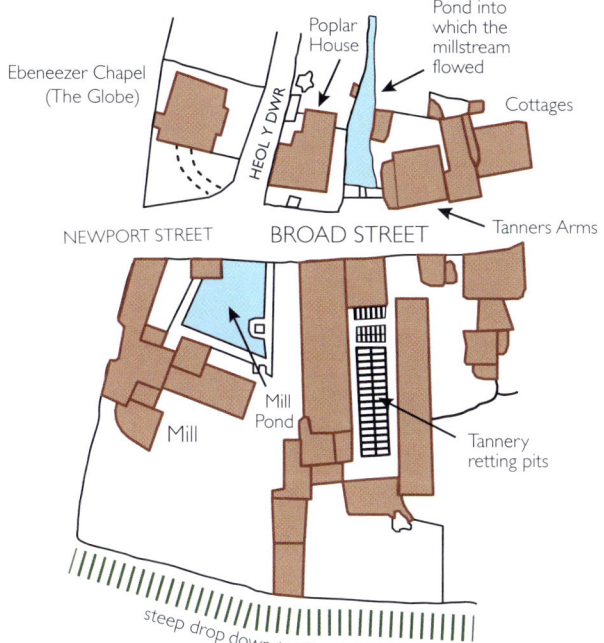

Plan of the Hay Mills in the nineteenth century, though the mill site is likely to have been much the same in Norman times. The long triangular pond into which the millstream flowed was piped under the road in two directions: one to the millpond and the other to the many small square retting pits of the tannery

used in tanning leather could thus be drained straight into the river.

Tanning was a long and complex process that involved animal hides being submerged in retting pits containing a variety of substances, which commonly included dog faeces and human urine. The contents of their chamber pots would have been a source of income for many of the townspeople. The prevailing wind is south-westerly, so the stench would have been blown away from the town and across the river – until the wind changed.

Leather was an essential commodity in Norman times. Saddles, bridles, harnesses, riding gaiters, blacksmith's aprons, jackets for hedgers, satchels and the protective jerkins worn by the common soldier would all have been made from the leather produced at this tannery. Even bottles. A manufactory on Heol y Dwr in later years would give the lower part of this road its one-time name of Leather Bottle Street.

A medieval house with shop front was usually protected by two horizontally hinged wooden shutters. These were barred at night but propped open in the day so that the top one gave shelter whilst the lower one provided a shelf for the display of goods. All items offered for sale would have been made locally, probably in a workshop behind the house or at the back of the shop itself. Leather goods were vital. Mr Vale, the saddler, would have a leather workshop on Broad Street in the 1930s and '40s and he could well have been at the end of a long tradition stretching back to the earliest Norman times.

The markets for cattle, sheep and poultry were held along the length of Broad Street in the road itself, where they were open to constant surveillance from the castle, since for many years there were few if any buildings in between. Farmers and their families would pour into town from the surrounding countryside, some in carts but many walking six or seven miles each way. Ale-houses and pie-sellers thrived.

Some of the animals brought into the market would have gone for immediate slaughter and there may well have been a slaughterhouse on Broad Street from the outset, as there would be until well into the twentieth century. Blood could drain from there down into the Wye. A slaughterhouse was the driving force behind a host of other industries in medieval Hay. Meat from the animals would go to a butcher's shop or the meat market, whilst the hides would go a few yards down the road to the tannery. The fat or tallow would go to the candle-makers and the horns to be carved into spoons and drinking horns. Parchment for writing paper was made from sheepskin, while knife handles were made from bone.

Considerable labour had gone into levelling the Broad Street burgage plots, but this had stopped once the far side of the road was reached. A raised, cobbled pavement was retained here, which could be used to line up items like eggs for sale, as from a market stall, and by the 1960s the practice of selling produce from here may well have been the oldest continuously maintained tradition in the town.

Miles of Gloucester

By 1135 Miles of Gloucester and his wife Sybil, daughter of Bernard de Neufmarché, were controlling the lordship of Brecon and much else besides. But there had been growing turbulence in the Marches throughout their marriage, and when Henry I died in 1135 this erupted into full-blown civil war.

Henry had named his daughter, the Empress Matilda, as his heir. But there were many who believed that women were unfit to occupy the throne and Miles was presumably among them, for initially he supported Matilda's cousin, Stephen. From the moment he met Matilda off the boat in 1139, however, he became devoted to her cause and she rewarded him well. In 1141, to the Forest of Dean and other properties she added the earldom of Hereford, first held by William FitzOsbern 70 years before.

He would not hold them for long, however, for on Christmas Eve 1143 he was shot through the heart in what may or may not have been a hunting accident in the Forest of Dean. It was a death strangely reminiscent of that of William Rufus in the New Forest.

Sybil donned a nun's habit and entered Llanthony Secunda Priory in Gloucester, once she had seen to it that her three daughters had all married advantageously – so advantageously in fact that Hay historian, Alan Nicholls, has been able to trace a line of descent from her down to Elizabeth II.[10]

Earl Roger

Miles was succeeded by each of his and Sybil's four sons in turn, and the eldest, Roger, earl of Hereford, seems to have taken a particular interest in Hay for he had several charters drawn up that make reference to the town.

The centre of the town seems to have been still largely open, although a church had clearly been built at St John's, for Earl Roger's first charter c.1144 mentions 'the land which lies near to the entrance of the church of St John outside the gates of the castle bailey'.[11] There were presumably gates at the foot of the steps down from the castle into the town and it sounds as if the land between there and St John's was still unbuilt on. St John's would at some stage become a Guild chapel.

The town was evidently thriving during Roger's lordship in spite of the ongoing war between Stephen and Matilda, for at some stage before his death in 1155 it became a borough. In England this would have required a royal charter but, as a Marcher lord, Roger had the power to grant the charter himself and it seems that he must have done so, for Hay is referred to as a borough from his time on.[12] Even more advantageously for the town, Roger seems to have set it up as a borough under the so-called Laws of Breteuil.[13]

William FitzOsbern had given Hereford a charter based on these Laws, which were actually a set of rare liberties and privileges first devised as a way of attracting settlers to his war-torn border town of Breteuil in Normandy. They were incorporated into Hereford's entry in Domesday Book and from then on Hereford was seen as a model borough throughout the Marches.[14] In marked contrast to the situation in England, where Norman lords were inflicting harsh injustices on their tenants without restraint, Marcher boroughs set up under the Laws of Breteuil gave their burgage holders an unusual degree of protection. The privilege most commonly taken advantage of, however, was the right to sublet burgages. Subletting left burgesses free to travel, which was unusual, as most people were not free to leave their homes at all under the feudal system. It also allowed burgesses to derive income from those burgages they were not occupying themselves.

The Marcher boroughs of Hereford, Cardiff, Builth, Brecon, Carmarthen, Ewyas Harold and Skenfrith, with perhaps nine or ten others, were established under the Laws of Breteuil. But if Hay was indeed one of them it is unusual in having survived without either expanding like Builth and Brecon, or contracting like Skenfrith.

The civil war finally came to an end with the death of Stephen. Henry II acceded to the throne in 1154 and Earl Roger entered Gloucester Abbey as a monk the following year. He died there a few months later and was succeeded by his three brothers, one after the other, all also dying without issue. Gerald of Wales says that they were all of inhuman cruelty, but does not say what led him to make that judgement. The last brother died in 1165 and the family holdings were then divided between his sisters, according to custom. Hay fell to a sister called Bertha, the fifth of Miles and Sybil's eight children to hold it.

WILLIAM AND MATILDA DE BRAOSE

The advantageous marriage Sybil had arranged for Bertha had linked her to the de Braose family,[15] originally from Briouze in Normandy. Bertha's husband was William de Braose, a close friend of Henry II and an eminent

Marcher lord. His father had extended the de Braose lands into Wales by conquering Radnor and Builth.

But it would be Bertha's son, another William, and his wife Matilda (Maud) de St Valery who would, in their different ways, make de Braose the name most readily associated with the early history of Hay. Matilda's name would even become the stuff of legend. Her story has been told many times, most notably by Hay resident, Barbara Erskine, in her fictionalised *The Lady of Hay*, and most recently by Hay historian, Peter Ford, in his *Matilda, Lady of Hay*.

William would become known as the Ogre of Abergavenny after an infamous occasion in 1175 when he invited a number of Welsh princes and leaders to dinner at Abergavenny Castle on Christmas Day, got them to leave their weapons outside, then closed the doors and had them all killed. This act of treachery was followed by the massacre of their now unprotected families, and Henry II was appalled.

A hundred years earlier the Normans had indulged in unbridled brutality towards both Welsh and English. Now the code of conduct known as chivalry had largely taken over and dealings with the nobility of subject nations were supposed to be honourable. Henry II withdrew his favour from the whole de Braose family and its name quickly became a byword for treachery and dishonour. William's father was deeply ashamed and, barred from the presence of his former friend, the king, retired to his Sussex estates where he died in 1179.

The leaders of Christendom were much occupied at this time by their desire to have Jerusalem under Christian control, and Henry II was one of the prime movers behind the Third Crusade. In 1188, therefore, the Archbishop of Canterbury, accompanied by Gerald of Wales, undertook a tour throughout Wales to drum up support, and in Hay they found a ready enthusiasm:

> We crossed the River Wye and made our way into Brecknockshire. After the sermon which was given in Hay, we saw a great number of men who wanted to take the cross come running towards the castle where the Archbishop was, leaving their cloaks behind in the hands of the wives and friends who had tried to hold them back.[16]

A readiness to fight had no doubt been fostered among the men of Hay by the training in arms they were required to undergo. Boys commonly received a crossbow on their fifth birthday and would practice until, by the time they were 14 or 15, they could draw the hefty instrument to its full extent and fire it accurately. In later years it would be the longbow. All men of fighting age were required to practice the use of these weapons on Sundays and Saints Days, and thus the lord, or lady, had a small army readily at his or her disposal.

The Third Crusade was to be a punishing and frustrating experience, however. The English contingent was led by Henry II's son, Richard (later the Lionheart), and the shallow-draught boats he used to convey his men to the Holy Land caused almost universal seasickness. Once they reached Jerusalem he twice turned his army back from besieging it, and on the second of these occasions they were, had he but realised it, on the eve of certain triumph. Prevented from achieving their aim and deprived of the spoils of victory, the survivors returned home thoroughly disillusioned.

Richard I died in 1199 and was succeeded by his brother, King John, who initially favoured William and Matilda de Braose. Twenty-five years had passed since the Massacre of Abergavenny, and John chose to forgive and forget, showering the couple with additional holdings that eventually took their Welsh lands as far as the Gower coast.

Hay castle had always been primarily a military building under the charge of a constable but Matilda de Braose – or Matilda de la Hay as King John called her – seems to have taken it as her residence for a time. She is said to have had 16 children but this did not, allegedly, stop her donning armour. On three occasions in the late 1190s she marched the men of Hay down Broad Street, across the Wye at the nearby ford, and on to do battle with the Welsh at Payen's castle (Painscastle) six miles away.

Hay had become an important trading centre by the year 1200,[17] perhaps as a result of Matilda's residence in the castle. Regular markets were held, and a highly successful Michaelmas fair. The church was rebuilt and enlarged around this time, suggesting an increase in population, and at least two more roads had become established. Bear Street followed that part of the town's southern edge not taken up by the castle, and Heol y Dwr (Water Street), with the mill stream flowing down one side of it, joined Bear Street to Broad Street.

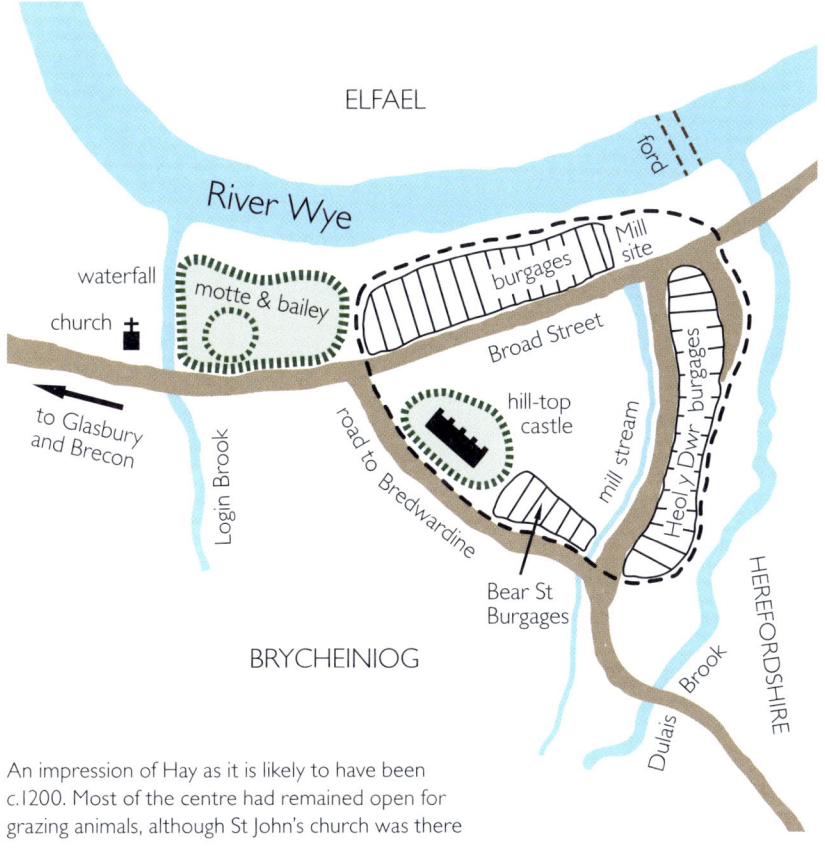

An impression of Hay as it is likely to have been c.1200. Most of the centre had remained open for grazing animals, although St John's church was there

Burgages were still on the outer side only, with much of the centre remaining open. The Church of St John was there (it had been mentioned in Earl Roger's charter c.1144), but most of the rest was probably still given over to grazing animals. They would be needed for food if the town were besieged.

The possibility of a Welsh attack certainly seems to have been on the mind of Matilda de Braose, for she made improvements to the castle in c.1200. No doubt she had been affected by her experiences at Painscastle. She is sometimes credited with having built the castle from scratch – and there was even a myth that, being a giantess, she achieved this single-handedly in one day. In reality, however, she seems to have blocked up the gates in the square stone gate-tower and added the arched gateway with portcullis that can be seen today. The curtain wall is also attributed to her.

An eighteenth-century engraving of Hay Castle, showing the keep and Matilda's gateway

Matilda's gateway from the south

The fall of William and Matilda de Braose from favour with King John was sudden and dramatic. Matilda is said to have revealed her knowledge of John having murdered his nephew, Arthur, and John retaliated sharply. In 1210 he incarcerated Matilda and her adult eldest son, William, in a royal castle variously said to have been either Windsor or Corfe, and deliberately starved them to death. William fled abroad and died there the following year.

John's inhuman treatment of the family added fuel to a fire that was already burning and would eventually spread into the flames of civil war. The barons had long been forced to suffer his rapacious megalomania, their wives and daughters subjected to his sexual assaults. Now he stood exposed as a murderer, described by a chronicler of the time as 'the very measure of human depravity'. In 1215 the barons forced him to put his seal on Magna Carta, but the Pope declared it null and void because it was issued under duress, and within a few months this great charter was worth less than the sheepskin parchment on which it was written.

That attempt to stem the tide of royal tyranny having failed, there was now open warfare. Some of the barons appealed to France for aid. But William and Matilda's two surviving sons, Giles and Reginald, allied themselves with Llewelyn ap Iorwerth, also known as Llewelyn the Great, and it drove John into one of the murderous rages for which he was famous. Shortly before he died in 1216 he ordered the castles of Hay and Radnor to be demolished and their townships put to the torch.[18]

The first major attack on Hay had not come from the Welsh, but from the King of England.

2

The Town Wall, the Burgage Holders and a Visiting Antiquary

Eva de Braose and the Town Wall

King John's chief adviser had been William Marshal, a man who, in the starkest possible contrast to John himself, was widely revered for his loyalty and integrity. His fighting skills were unparalleled and this, combined with a lifetime of chivalrous conduct, had gained him a reputation as the greatest knight in Europe. He had remained loyal to John even through the worst of that monarch's unpredictable rages.

He was in his 70th year when John died in 1216, leaving the country in chaos, but all eyes turned to him nonetheless. Half the kingdom, including London, had been lost to Prince Louis of France and two-thirds of the English barons were supporting him. The choice before William Marshal was therefore stark. He could hold to his lifelong principle of loyalty to the Crown and risk losing everything he had. Or he could abandon his principles and side with the majority of the barons. The future of his large family, his castle at Chepstow and his earldoms of Leicester and Pembroke were all at stake. But he chose loyalty, and rode to meet John's nine-year-old son, now Henry III, a boy who was so frail that he had to be carried to the meeting by a man-at-arms. Things would have gone badly for Henry if William Marshal had not taken his part and he must have known it. 'I deliver myself up to God and to you', he is reported to have said when they met, and it was a wise move. William Marshal was made Regent and Protector and fought a vigorous campaign on the boy's behalf.

One of Marshal's first acts, once Henry was secure on his throne, was to issue a new version of Magna Carta; a version more readily acceptable to the autocratic sensibilities of kings and popes, and therefore more likely to endure. Henry III confirmed it when he came of age in 1225 and it has become the foundation of both the British and the American constitutions.

William Marshal's connection with Hay came through the eighth of his ten children, a lively, high-spirited girl called Eva. She married William v de Braose, son of Reginald and grandson of Matilda, and had many of his lands, including Hay, assigned to her when he died. The castles, however, were initially exempted. These passed into the wardship of her brother, another William Marshal, and when he died in 1231 to a highly unpopular official in Henry III's court called Hubert de Burgh. The two William Marshals, father and son, had maintained cordial relations with the Welsh, but Hubert de Burgh was actively hostile.

Henry III spent much of the summer of 1231 supervising the rebuilding of castles in Wales. He even spent a few days with his retinue in Hay to oversee the rebuilding of the castle that his father, King John, had sacked.[1] To the Welsh leader Llewelyn ap Iorwerth, Llewelyn the Great, however, all this was sheer provocation and in that same year he 'laid waste Montgomery, Brecon and Hay, with Radnor Castle, by pillage and fire'.[2]

The town had now been sacked twice within 15 years, and it was clear that something needed to be done about its defences.

It might have been assumed that, being in effect an outer bailey to Hay Castle, the town would have been walled round from the beginning, but that was not the case. Perhaps, given that the name La Haye is usually translated as 'the hedged enclosure', it had indeed been protected by a large hedge running along the top of the riverbank at the far end of the Belmont Road/ Broad Street burgages, and then behind those of Heol y Dwr and Bear Street. Whatever form the early protection had taken, however, it was about to be replaced by a wall.

Henry III owed his throne to William Marshal, and he seems to have had considerable respect for Marshal's daughter, Eva de Braose. Another of her brothers, Richard Marshal, rebelled in 1234 but Henry allowed Eva safe conduct to act as arbiter, and on the successful completion of the arbitration issued a formal statement declaring that she had been 'received back into his grace'. He ordered the 'castle and all the land of Hay with all the stock therein' to be delivered into her own hands, and on 30 June he himself visited her at Hay Castle, his second visit to the town. Nine months later, on 20 March 1235, she was granted 12 marks for strengthening the fortifications of her town of Hay.[3] But it was by no means enough to make the town secure. More money was needed, and two years later, in March 1237, she was granted the right to levy a murage tax, payable once a week for three years, to be used for the building of a wall round the town.[4] Matilda de Braose had given the castle its curtain wall and gateway with portcullis; Eva de Braose would give the town its wall.

The town would not prove impregnable, however, even with a two-metre thick wall round it, and less than 30 years after the wall was completed castle and town were 'reduced' by Simon de Montfort, 5th earl of Leicester. The conflagration instigated by his rebellion of 1265 covered much of England and the whole of the Marches because Henry III, like his father King John before him, had over-reached himself and provoked his barons to rebellion. Simon de Montfort, like William Marshal, is today regarded as one of the great progenitors of parliamentary democracy.

The lofty walls of Hay would remain its most striking feature for centuries, in spite of repeated attacks on the town. Encircling the top of the hill, they made a forcible impression on those approaching, particularly from the north from where they could be seen towering above the Wye. Even from the south where the land stretches away to the Black Mountains, the walls of Hay could be seen rising 50 feet either side of the castle's inner bailey.[5] And to the east, a visitor would remark as late as 1883 that: 'A considerable portion of the town wall still remains on the eastern side of the town, and forms a conspicuous object from the railway station'.[6]

❖❖❖

THE TOWN WALL

There were three gates in the town wall: one at each of the three corners of its roughly triangular shape. Two of these were at either end of the Newport Street–Broad Street–Belmont Road continuum, for centuries the main route from Clifford to Glasbury. The other was across what is now Lion Street outside the Drill Hall, close by the Black Lion.

A considerable portion of the town wall still exists on the eastern side of the town, though it has been much rebuilt over the years, and today is largely obscured by vegetation. Three-storey modern houses now rise above it. A narrow footpath runs beside its base, fenced off from a field called the Newports.

The town wall in Booth Gardens. This is one of the few places where the wall is not now obscured by vegetation

At the top of Belmont Road, where the western gate once stood, the western edge of the town wall followed the line of the footpath that runs down to the top of the riverbank from the archway (beside Jones Home Hardware).

The wall is still just visible at the far end of this path, and at one time it ran from here along the end of the Belmont Road/ Broad Street burgages. It was partially dismantled when the railway was constructed on a terrace along the river bank in 1864.

◆◆

The Burgage Holders of 1340

In the Glamorgan Record Office at Cardiff, there is a document dated 1340,[7] which gives, for the first time, the names of Hay's burgage holders, and it makes interesting reading:

Likewise any notwithstanding the law of the march. John Brouugh, John Walwayn, the chaplain of the Blessed Mary, John Walwayn, Philip Scut, and Matthew Goch 1 burgage each for 12d. each; Alice Attebroke 2 burgages for 2s.; the chaplain of the Blessed Mary, Edith Benerch, and John Bonman 1 burgage each for 12d. each; Philip Scut 2 burgages for 2s. and part of a strip for 1d.; the chaplain of the Blessed Mary 1 burgage for 12d. and part of a strip for 1d.; Agnes Walweyn 1 burgage for 12d.; Robert Prophet 5 burgages for 2s.6d. and 1 strip for 1d.; Agnes Walweyn 1 burgage for 12d.; John Wallewayn 2 burgages for 2s. and part of a strip for 1d.; William Bengemne 1 burgage for 12d.; and part of a strip for 1d.; Agnes Wallewayn 1 burgage for 12d. and part of a strip for 1d.; Thomas Bongham 3 burgages for 3s. and 1 strip for 2d. John Wallewayn 5 burgages for 5s., 1 strip for 2d. and 1 burgage of the fee of William Waldeboef for 1d. at Michaelmas; Thomas Dun 4 burgages for 4s. and 1 strip for 1d.; Richard Wallewayn 4 burgages for 4s.; Agnes Wallewayn 1 burgage for 12d. and 2 burgages for 2s.; Walter le Baker and the chaplain of the Blessed Mary 2 burgages each for 2s.; John son of William and Thomas Bongham 1 burgage each for 12d. each; Agnes Wallewayn 2 burgages for 2s.; Thomas Dun' and Agnes Wallewayn 1 burgage each for 12d. each; Philip Budell ½ burgage for 6d. Alice Wallewayn 1½ burgages for 18d.; Philip Budell 1½ burgages for 18d.; John de Lulham 5 burgages for 5s.; Robert de Homme 2 burgages for 2s.; Roger the miller, William Bengemme, and the chaplain of the Blessed Mary 1 burgage each for 12d. each; Philip Budell 2 burgages for 2s.; and Elyas Wolf 1 burgage for 12d. All holding as said John Gille.

The information in this document was given by a certain John Gille, who seems to have gone from one burgage plot to the next in his mind all round the town. To find out how many burgages there were, therefore, and how many burgesses, it is necessary to count them up. In the variant of the document given above there are 79 burgages, held by only 21 burgesses, so it looks as if the freedom to sublet under the Laws of Breteuil was being extensively enjoyed.

If John Gille was indeed going round the town from one plot to the next in his mind, then the burgage holders of Broad Street are given in order somewhere in his list, though it is not possible to know which they are. The rest would have been from Belmont Road, Bear Street and Heol y Dwr. The Anglo-Norman name Wallewayn, or Walwyn, occurs throughout the list, however, so either John, or Richard, or Alice Walwyn must have lived on Broad Street.

Five of the burgesses, including John Gille, have a French surname. Possibly their ancestors had been brought over from Normandy to provide the necessary expertise in castle-building since castles – at least in the Norman sense – were unknown in Britain before the Conquest. Hereford also is known to have had a small number of French burgesses.

There are no Welsh names in the list for Welsh men and women were disbarred from holding burgages. It was racial discrimination of this kind, and worse, that would later fuel the rebellion of Owain Glyndŵr.

John Gille appears to have held some office in the town, perhaps as reeve, which was roughly equivalent to mayor. His duties are clearly listed:

> John Gille holds 2½ burgages from the lord for himself and heirs and owes suit at 3 lawful hundred courts without summons and shall come to a
> day of the march for the hundred and lord's court for 3 days if he is in the lordship. If fit (sanus) and in the town he shall come to the hue and cry in the town, if he should hear it, and in the lordship with the steward or his lieutenant whenever it is commanded or shall be amerced 12d. in the lord's court. If summoned he shall go with the lord or his lieutenant at his own costs within the lordship wherever the lord wishes for 1 day. If the lord wishes to have him longer or outside the lordship then he shall be at the lord's pledge. He shall be portreeve, catchpole or ale-taster if elected. He shall give the lord ... ale from which he brews. He shall do suit to the lord's mill, bake his bread at the lord's oven, help lead the water of the Duueleis when necessary to the said mill, and shall pay 2s.6d. at the Annunciation and Michaelmas yearly.

The Black Death

If there were 79 burgages in Hay in 1340, however, this number seems to have more than doubled within the following 20 years,[8] though the reason for this sudden expansion has not been established. Possibly it was occasioned by an influx of people seeking refuge from the plague.

The Black Death first hit the south coast of England in July 1348, and within 18 months had spread over the whole of England and Wales. Some places lost 80% of their population. Hay was spared both this and the second wave of the pandemic, however, probably because it was not on any of the main trading routes. It took a third outbreak, in 1369, for the Hay area to be affected.

The short-term effects of this deadly disease were harsh and horrible, the suffering appalling. By the end of all three outbreaks the population of Wales had been reduced from something like 300,000 to under 200,000.

There were some long-term benefits, however. Wages improved significantly as the shortage of manpower enabled agricultural workers to name the price of their labour. The old feudal system was giving way to a money economy. Standards of living rose, and the diet of peasants in 1430 was better than that of many army recruits in 1914.

In the Hay area there was a partial shift away from labour-intensive agriculture towards more sheep and dairy farming. Now the famous Hereford beef cattle could be found in the hinterland, and were no doubt offered for sale in Broad Street's markets. And increased supplies of Welsh wool gave a boost to Hay's flannel industry.

The flannel industry had been brought to Wales long before by Cistercian monks from the Continent, and was by this time a mainstay of the Welsh economy. The fine, soft quality of Welsh wool made it ideal for wearing next to the skin once it had been through the fulling process, and by 1372, just three years after the third outbreak of the Black Death, there seem to have been two fulling mills in Hay. The manor had passed temporarily into the hands of Edward III and he was drawing the rents:

> The burgage rents, common oven, stalls of the fairs and markets of the town were let at £40, two watermills with the fishing in the millpool at £9 6s 8d and a fulling mill at £1 6s 8d ... the Wye ferry £1 6s 8d.[9]

The suggestion here is that two water mills were running off the millpond on the Broad Street mill site, with a fulling mill perhaps somewhere else. This was possibly on Heol y Dwr. There was an old Tuck Mill on the lower part of this street in 1902[10] ('tucking' is a West Country word for fulling).

It is likely, however, that the lower of the two mills on the Broad Street mill site was also used for fulling at this time. The noxious wastewater could then be discharged straight into the Wye, as it was from the tannery.

◆◆◆

FULLING

Fulling was basically a process for turning lengths of un-dyed woollen cloth into flannel so that it lost its oiliness and was smooth enough to be worn next to the skin. The process tightened the weave so as to make the material not only smoother but stronger, less liable to fray, warm to wear – and, importantly for many, able to absorb sweat. Working people would use flannel for men's shirts, usually with a double thickness over the shoulders. It was also used for nightshirts, women's red flannel petticoats and much else. In very cold weather outdoor workers would often have an extra strip of flannel warmed in front of the fire and wound round their chests under a flannel shirt to protect against bronchitis.

The process of fulling was an ingenious one by which sheep sweat (up to eight per cent of the original weight of the fleece) and the wool's natural oiliness were removed at the same time as all the little barbs in the wool that make it itchy to wear were linked together like Velcro to make the fabric smooth. This double process was achieved by pounding the woollen cloth with wooden hammers whilst it was immersed in a solution containing, among other things, stale urine (ammonia) and fuller's earth. Tappets on the turning axle lifted the hammers and released them in sequence so that the cloth was hammered evenly in a process as noisy as it was effective. Fullers were skilled workers earning up to three times the wages of an agricultural labourer.

Once the fulling process was completed the flannel would be stretched over tenterhooks in the open air and left to dry.

◆◆◆

The End of the Great Marcher Lordships

Throughout most of 1404 Hay Castle was under the command of Sir John Oldcastle, the man on whom Shakespeare based his character, Falstaff.[11] But in 1405 town and castle were laid waste, to some extent, during the uprising led by the legendary Welsh leader, Owain Glyndŵr. The Welsh wanted an end to the institutionalised racism that barred them from playing any part in the governance of their own country, and to have Wales back as a free and independent nation. Glyndŵr's attack on the town would go down in history as having 'laid it in ashes'[12] – though Hay historian, Geoffrey Fairs, has cast doubt on this. He suggests that Glyndŵr may have had supporters within the town who saved it from extensive devastation.

But Hay would remain subject to constant attack, even once Glyndŵr's uprising was over. On the other side of the Wye was the land of Elfael whose men were relentless in making raids on Hay, though some of these were relatively trivial, as when the doves were stolen from the lord's dovecote. It was as if the young bucks were daring each other to cross the river, invade the walled town, and bring back some evidence of success. At one point the ferry was holed, presumably to prevent pursuit. But some of the raids were more serious, and in 1450 some 90 men were summoned from English and Welsh Hay combined to take up arms 'for the defence and safe keeping of the town for fourteen days and nights against the enemies from the Lord of Elfael'.[13]

The raids continued well into the Tudor period until, finally, Henry VIII's chief advisor, Thomas Cromwell, put his lawyer's mind to the whole problem of conflict in the Marches and came up with a radical solution. The great Marcher lordships, he concluded, should be abolished altogether, and in 1535 he instigated the Laws in Wales Acts, which brought the whole of the March under civil rather than military authority. Two new counties were created in the Hay area. Breconshire replaced the old lordship of Brecon, and on the other side of the Wye the land of Elfael was absorbed into the new county of Radnorshire. Hay was at the point where these two met with Herefordshire, and was thus at the outermost tip of all three.

Cromwell's changeover was not effected painlessly, however, for some 5,000 people were hanged in the course of the transition by the newly-appointed

Lord President of the Council in the Marches of Wales, the fearsome and fanatical Rowland Lee, Bishop of Coventry and Lichfield. Cromwell had instructed him to bring the whole of the March into a uniform state of law and order and he carried out the brief with great gusto, torturing and hanging those considered at fault, and sparing neither the common people nor the nobility. It was a brutal but effective way of clearing the ground for the next stage of Cromwell and Henry VIII's plan for Wales. The Act of Union of England and Wales defined it clearly:

> Wales shall be, stand and continue for ever from henceforth incorporated, united and annexed to and with this his Realm of England.[14]

It was very far from the solution that Owain Glyndŵr had wanted. His fight had been for a free and independent Wales. But it satisfied the Welsh gentry to a large extent for they now had parity with their counterparts in England. And it brought peace to the Marches. Hay would not be sacked, or even attacked, again.

John Leland

One of the first travellers to benefit from the newly peaceable conditions in the Marches was a young antiquarian called John Leland. Late one summer evening in 1538, or thereabouts, he rode over the hill from Clyro and crossed the River Wye at the ford. 'I cam in crepusculo to the Hay', he wrote in his notebook, 'I came at dusk to the Hay', and he goes on to give the earliest first-hand impression that we have of the town.

He had travelled from Old Radnor and was on his way to Brecon, making notes as he went, for he was aiming at something that had never been attempted before – the compilation of a gazetteer of all the towns and villages in England and Wales. The condition of the roads was such as to discourage most people from unnecessary travel, yet in the six summers between 1536 and 1542 Leland somehow managed to cover virtually the whole of England and Wales, apart from the wetlands of East Anglia. It was a huge achievement. Alone and on horseback, he negotiated hundreds of miles of roads that were little more than cart tracks, hopelessly muddy in wet weather and deeply rutted when dry. Even the main highways were unpaved. Local people might fill the worst of the holes with crushed rocks or gravel but these soon sank under the mud. Very few people travelled any distance from home.

Not all Leland's travels were purely to collect information for his own purposes, however. Some of the visits he made along the way were on behalf of the king. Back in 1533 Henry VIII had commissioned him to examine the libraries of all the monasteries and colleges in England, and this had given him an unparalleled appreciation of the country's literary heritage. It had caused him considerable distress then, when the First Suppression Act of 1536 had closed all the smaller monasteries. German scholars, he complained to his patron, Thomas Cromwell, were routinely taking advantage of the situation to remove important books and manuscripts from the libraries of these monasteries and claim them as 'monuments of their own country'.

Cromwell and the king devised a partial remedy. They ordered a complete reorganisation of the royal library, then housed in the great palaces of Hampton Court, Greenwich and Whitehall, so that many more books could be accommodated. Then, as Cromwell's blend of bribery and intimidation brought down the larger monastic houses, Leland was authorised to continue his travels and dispatch the most important of their books and manuscripts back to London. Four hundred and fifty or so years into the future Richard Booth, bookshop owner and self-styled 'King of Hay', would also travel round the country collecting up books from libraries that were being disbanded.

Most of Leland's notes on the places he visited are short and purely factual. They read as if made in response to a mental checklist. Has the place a castle? Who owns it? Is there a bridge? How many arches has it? and so on. When he got to Hay, however, he made an exception and gives some engagingly personal details.

> When I approchid nere the Hay, and began to discend from thens I saw on the hither side of the Wy a good mile from the Hay the castel of Clereho. After passing over Wy River, the which for lak of good knowleg yn me of the fourde did sore troble my horse, I cam in crepusculo to the Hay.[15]

It is rare for Leland to mention either himself or his horse, but the ford seems to have caused him particular trouble. The Wye is wide at this point and the ford may have been divided into sections by islands, or at least one island. With the route across far from clear in a dim light, we can imagine him struggling to find it after a long day on the road, his horse floundering in the water, his own feet and legs drenched.

> The Hay stondith hard apon Wy, and yet sheuith the token of a right strong waulle, having in hit iii gates and a posterne. Ther is also a castel, the which sumtime hath bene right stately.

Once across, he and his bedraggled horse would have trudged up the track that is now Wyeford Road and turned right to come immediately upon the Water Gate in the town wall. It must have been still in place then, if not in use, for as late as 1831 a writer would remark that the town gates had been removed within living memory.[16] His weary horse then had the short but steep incline of Watergate Street (now Newport Street) ahead and perhaps Leland took pity on the animal and dismounted, walking with it to the top and passing the mill pond and the mill to find himself on Broad Street in the growing dark.

The Three Tuns and Old House (No. 3) began as a single dwelling, rebuilt c.1600

Past the mill pond was an early Tudor timber-framed house, some 30 years old at the time, on the corner of an entryway. The house would be rebuilt in around 1600, and at some stage after that divided into an alehouse called the Spreadeagle (now the Three Tuns) and a private dwelling, now called Old House. The entryway would eventually become Bridge Street, but in Leland's time it was blocked at the far end by the town wall and led only to stables. Leland must have spent the night in Hay, for he says that he went to Mass the following day, but he gives no clue as to where he stayed.

> Within the toune is but one poore paroche. In the suburbe hard by Wy is a paroche chirch meately fair. Ther is also in the suburbe a chapel wher on a Sunday I hard Messe.

He appears to have eschewed St Mary's Church for a chapel somewhere in the 'suburb', which was a settlement round the church known as Weston[17] – and been puzzled by the presence of the nearby motte:

> Not far from the paroche chirch in the suburbe is a great rounde hill of yearth cast up by mennes hondes other for a wynd mille to stond apon, or rather for sum fortres of bataille.
>
> The toun of the Hay hath yet a market, but the toun within the waulles is wondrously decaied. The ruin is ascribed to Oene Glindour.

Leland had arrived in Hay to find the town semi-derelict. As noted above, Geoffrey Fairs has cast doubt on how much damage was actually done by the Glyndŵr rebellion of 1405, but there had been many other attacks in the intervening years. Leland's belief that much of the town had been 'wondrously decaied' for the previous 130 years is interesting, however. It conjures images of ruins covered by ivy and other vegetation, with sizeable trees growing up through the cracks. But that cannot have been the whole story. The Tudor house on Broad Street had been built in the previous 30 years, markets were still being held, and the mill is likely to have been in operation.

> One shewid me in the town the ruines of a gentilman's place caulid Waulwine, be whose meanes Prince Lluelin was sodenli taken at Buelth Castel, and ther beheddid, and his hedde sent to the Kinge.

There was at least one house lying in ruins, however. The gentleman called Waulwine was a certain Sir Elias Walwyn who had headed the detachment of soldiers that won the final battle against Prince Llewelyn ap Gruffydd, in 1282. Also known as Llewelyn the Last, the latter was the last sovereign Prince of Wales, and grandson to Llewelyn the Great who had burned Hay Castle in 1231. After fleeing the battlefield, he had been killed by an unknown soldier at Aberedw rocks near Builth Wells, his head cut off and sent to Edward I in London to be displayed as a trophy symbolising the English king's triumph over Wales. It seems then that the last sovereign Prince of Wales was defeated by someone who lived in Hay, and quite probably in one of the larger burgage houses on Broad Street.

> Duless a prety river rising in the montannes about iii myles from Hay cummeth even thorough the toun, and strait into Wy without the est gate of the town. In feldes hard by in ploughyng hath be founde offtimes numismata Romanorum, the wich ther communely be cauuled the Jewis mony.

In saying that Roman coins had often turned up in the course of ploughing nearby fields, Leland is probably referring to the site of the Roman fort at Boatside on the other side of the Wye. Recent excavations there have yielded little, however, and certainly no coins. The largest object recovered has been a donkey mill, which was a large stone quern turned by either a donkey or in some cases a slave. This is presently on loan to St Fagan's Museum outside Cardiff.

Elsewhere, Leland refers to 'antique money' discovered beside Hay Castle, though he does not say it was Roman. It was found, he says, with pots and other notable things beside the ruins of the wall of an earlier town that was by then 'clean desolated'. He says:

> At Hay owt of Herfordshire beside the castel, as they say, apere the ruines of a wal of a town. Ther is much antique mony fownd, and pottes with other notable thingges. Wher appere any tokins of great old townes now clene desolated.[18]

If the ruins of the wall of this mysterious former town were to be seen in Leland's time, however, they are not recorded as having been seen since.

> The toune longgid to the Duke of Bokingham. It perteinith now to the Lord Staford his sonne.

The dukes of Buckingham were the last of the Marcher lords to rule in the Hay area. They were all vastly wealthy, though none of their money ever trickled down to the impoverished town. Leland is referring here to the third duke, sometimes known as 'Proud Buckingham'. His claim to the throne being somewhat better than the king's own, Henry VIII saw him as a threat and in 1521 had him executed on trumped-up charges of treason. The Buckingham estates were eventually restored to his son but Lord Stafford would never have anything like the power or influence his forbears had enjoyed. The days of the great Marcher lords were over.

> Artures Hille, and summe other of the banknes veri manifestly apere to a man loking out of the west gate of Hay.

The final sentence of Leland's section on Hay provides us with something of a mystery, for 'Arthur's Hill' cannot now be identified.

Leland might perhaps have managed to publish his gazetteer if he had confined himself to that one project, ambitious though it was. But he also had a number of other grand ideas, and the volume of work he set himself became overwhelming. Tragically, he spent the last years of his life certified as insane under the care of his brother in London, and died in his late forties, in April 1552, 12 years after the dramatic downfall of his patron, Thomas Cromwell. The notes for his gazetteer would remain unpublished until Victorian times. Today they are generally found in five volumes usually referred to as *Leland's Itinerary*.

James Boyle

Hay had been 'wondrously dec'aied' for a long time before Leland's visit in the late 1530s and would remain in a state of semi-dereliction for long after it. The castle also continued to decline and in 1542, some four years after Leland's visit, it was decommissioned as a military establishment. It was now redundant, and shortly before he died in 1547, Henry VIII granted it 'by some irregular means' to a dubious character called James Boyle, who also became Lord of the Manor, and Boyle commissioned a certain amount of rebuilding, the remnant of which now forms the small Elizabethan section of Hay Castle.

His tenure as Lord of the Manor would last 50 inglorious years during which the fabric of the town would largely continue to decay while its population suffered a range of indignities. Fairs and markets were disrupted by violence, Boyle's bailiff being an officious, violent man who seems to have killed at least one pedlar. Boyle himself was fined on more than one occasion for the illegal collection of tolls.[19]

James Boyle died sometime around 1600 but he had set a precedent, for his successor, his grandson-in-law, Howell Gwynn IV of Trecastle, was also prosecuted for the extortion of overly large tolls.[20] His tenure would also last for some 50 years, but from the death of James Boyle onwards Hay would begin to thrive in spite of the illegal tolls. The old queen, Elizabeth I, died in 1603. James I brought his young family down from Scotland and a wave of optimism spread throughout the kingdom. Hay found a new community spirit, its markets obtained a fresh lease of life, and a spate of building began that would continue intermittently throughout the century.

3

Broad Street Houses, a Jacobean Mansion and the first Bridge

THE seventeenth century would see much building, or rebuilding, in Hay.

The Tudor house that Leland passed (now the Three Tuns and Old House) was partially rebuilt in the year 1600 and this was followed by a whole spate of new building on Broad Street.

No. 6 carries the date 1623 on the front and is one of the few houses in this part of Wales that has timber-framing exposed to view. With a timber-framed front and the other three walls of stone, it is a humble member of a class widespread in northern Europe and known in Holland as the 'three-quarter house'.[1] The Black Swan next door is of a not dissimilar age.

Further down the street, an earlier version of No. 14 seems to have been built around this time, for a stone from it, inscribed '1633 March 24', was incorporated into the present Victorian rebuild of 1886.[2] Its footprint is small by comparison to No. 6 and it seems to have been stone-built, as opposed to the timber-framing favoured by the more prosperous burgesses of the town.

The dates of other buildings erected on Broad Street around this time are less certain. The Rose and Crown is thought to date from sometime in the seventeenth century; while the Seven Stars and No. 12 next door to it are both thought to have seventeenth-century timber-framed origins. Tinto House would come later, in the early to mid eighteenth century.[3]

On the other side of the road only the back part of West House and No. 22, and the Boardroom date from the seventeenth century or before, although there was an earlier building where Bank House stands now. Most of the southern side may have remained open for another century or so.

The Cheese Market replaced a Tudor market hall built on much the same pattern by the people of Hay. The statue on the end wall is of Henry VII, the first Welsh King of England.

Parts of the rest of the town would also become built-up during the seventeenth century, with an emphasis on houses that doubled as shops. High Town, Market Street and Lion Street each have one or two buildings dating from that century, and by 1684 there must also have been houses on Castle Street, for their roofs appear in a drawing from that date.[4]

The trading life of the town was given a major boost when the use of its Tudor market hall was recovered. Built by the people of Hay themselves but illegally rented out for private gain under James Boyle, it was now restored to its proper use following a petition to the Court of Star Chamber. It appears to have been similar in form to the present Cheese Market and on the same site, with rooms above a colonnaded market area where traders could stand 'and vend with their corn, grain, victuals and commodities'.[5] Hay had become the chief corn market of Breconshire by 1631 and the recovery of its market hall had no doubt played some part in this. Hay was on the eastern edge of Breconshire so its pre-eminence in the field of buying and selling corn was presumably due to trading between the three counties of Herefordshire, Radnorshire and Breconshire, all of which met at Hay.

The town as a whole would remain relatively undeveloped for at least another century, however. As late as 1808 a writer would claim that 'the town consists of one street, dividing into a fork near the middle as we proceed eastward'. And 'The houses, only a few excepted, are very indifferent habitations, and much scattered.'[6]

Howell Gwynn builds a Mansion c.1636

Up at the castle, Howell Gwynn was joining in the building craze of the early seventeenth century by erecting a brand new mansion alongside his father-in-law's Elizabethan addition to the Norman keep and gateway. Dendrochronology has shown that its oldest timbers come from a tree felled in 1636, and recent archaeology has found that he had somehow managed to incorporate the remains of a huge Norman wall. For some reason that remains unclear, he raised the ground level by two metres before laying the ground floor.

A photograph from towards the end of the nineteenth century, showing the south front of the Jacobean mansion and the carriage sweep

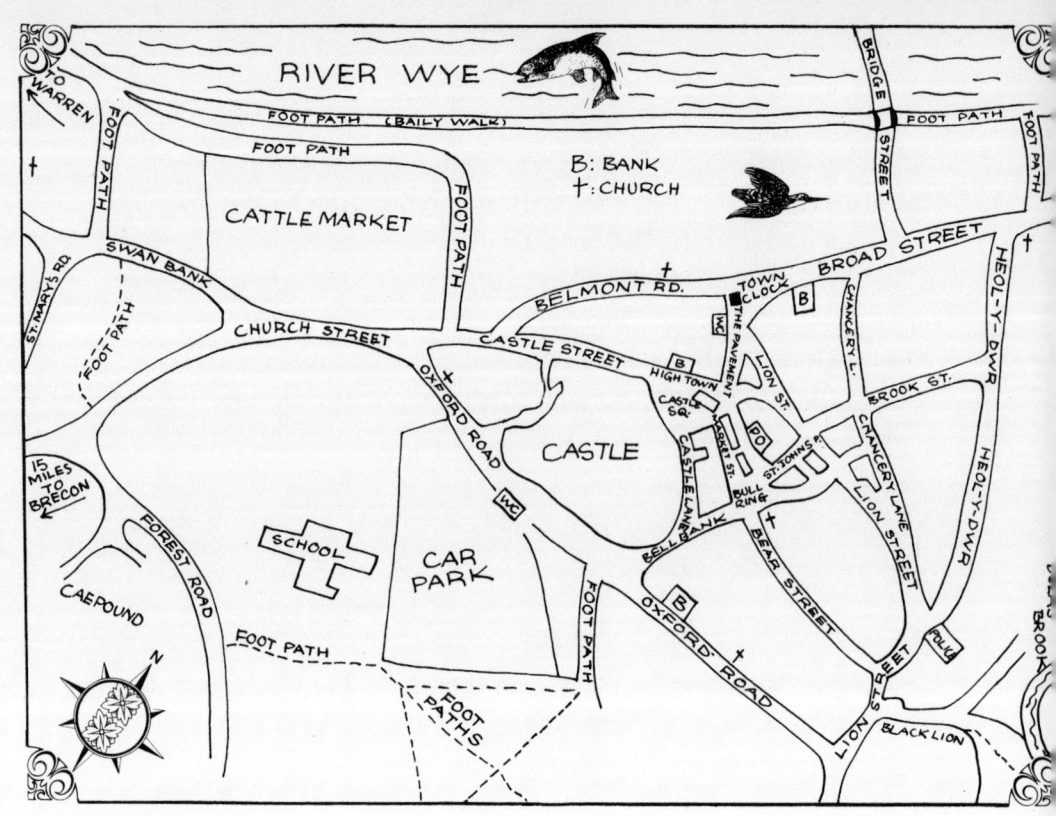

Map of Hay, from *Grant's Guide to Hay-on-Wye*, by David Cooke & John Grant (Hay, 1981)

Sensibly, this grand dwelling turned its back on the town, for entry from that direction is very steep, whereas an entrance from Oxford Road could be gracious. Visitors were greeted by lawns, with a view across to Hay Bluff and the Black Mountains, and a carriage sweep made it possible for vehicles to turn round. It could legitimately have been called The Manor House, since Gwynn was Lord of the Manor, but in fact it has always been known, together with the Norman and Elizabethen parts, simply as Hay Castle.

Thomas Dineley, 1684

If John Leland was the Tudor antiquarian who recorded his impressions of Hay, his Stuart equivalent 125 years later was Thomas Dineley. Unlike Leland, who had arrived at dusk alone, weary and dishevelled, Dineley arrived with some ceremony, for he was travelling with a member of the aristocracy.

Henry Somerset had been created 1st duke of Beaufort two years earlier by Charles II and now, in 1684, was on a grand progress throughout Wales in his capacity as Lord President of the Council of Wales, and Lord Warden of the Marches.[7] Dineley kept a diary during the progress, with sketches, but once the journey was over this was lodged in the Beaufort archives and lay there unregarded for the next 200 years. It took the publication of a facsimile in 1888[8] to bring it to the attention of the public and make it widely available.

The duke was met at Whitney-on-Wye, beyond Clifford, and escorted to 'the Haye' with considerable pomp and ceremony. He was riding, says Thomas Dineley, in a chariot (a light, four-wheeled carriage used for ceremonial occasions), and was met by the High Sheriff of Brecon with Gentlemen and County troop in attendance. From Whitney the procession would have taken the lower Clifford road to Hay, crossing the Dulais at the foot of Watergate (Newport) Street and coming up onto Broad Street, much as William FitzOsbern had done 500 years before. The visit had no doubt been planned to avoid market day, or the duke's chariot would have had to contend with a street full of sheep and cattle.

The duke was to be entertained at Hay Castle by Elizabeth Gwynn, granddaughter of the now long-dead Howell Gwynn, and remembered today largely on account of the almshouses she would found in 1699. The best way to get to the castle from Broad Street in a chariot was via Belmont Road, then variously called Lean Street or Back Lane,[9] which, although narrow, was still easier to negotiate then a winding route through the centre of town. From the top it was a matter of turning left where the Blue Boar now stands before sweeping in through the gateway of the castle, so angled as to make entry from this direction the only feasible one for larger carriages.

The duke and his entourage were given dinner followed by 'a very handsome Entertainment', and the duke himself no doubt spent the night at the castle. Dineley, however, was of relatively humble stock, his father being controller of customs at Southampton, and it is possible that he stayed at the Black Swan on Broad Street for it is the only building he names apart from the schoolhouse and the castle.

The sketch that Dineley made of the schoolhouse (St John's) has a banner heading that reads: 'THE FACE OF THE SCHOOL HOUSE AT THE HAY TOWARDS THE BLACK SWAN', with an extra bit that looks as if it says 'I AN HERE'.

CXLII.

IN HOPE OF A IOYFUL RESURRECTION HERE LIETH THE BODY OF
IANE THE WIFE OF IAMES WILLIAMS OF THE GREEN=PITT MAWRE
WHO DEPARTED THIS LIFE THE XXV DAY OF IANVARY. M.DC.LXXIV.

The descendents from S.r Roger Vaughan of Tretour in the County of Brecknock Kent have (as frequently seen in this Town) for Arms Sable 3 Infants heads couped at the shoulder each with a Snake about the neck all proper, it is otherwise born by S.r Charles Resp page 80 See Bristol.

In a fair Pedigree in the hands of Edw. Gwin of Hereford Esq.r Counsellor at Law I find that Howel Gwyn of Trecastle in the County of Brecon Esq.r was lineally descended both by Father and Mother off and from V KINGS, I DUKE and VII EARLES As set forth by Thomas Jones at FOUNTAINE GATE EDWARD I, PHILIP of FRANCE EDWARD II & the III.d of ENGLAND PETER KING OF SPAIN
E.DM LANGLEY D. of YORK E.DM E. of WOODSTOCK W.m E. of HENAULT & KENT
S.r THOMAS HOLLAND E. of KENT y.e same Arms as y.e of Woodstock in Right of his wife. E.DM HOLLAND Earle of KENT y.e same Coat QUINCY Earle of WINCHESTER Mars, 7 Mascles Sol. 3.3.&1.
Vayre Sol & Mars
WILLIAM Earle Marshal of Engl.
E. PENBROKE & OGNY
Besides from various Lords as AUDELEY, IN L.d WAKE, W.m E. of Barry & Kinor d of Lug
E. FERRARS & CHARTLEY
GWYN. Brychi Lord of Brec.
The quarterings with Gwyn are Reremice or Batts displaied.
This had 30 Children Many of his sonnes were Lords of great Provinces and his daughters wives to great Princes and all the rest that were not married were religious and are numbred among the Saynts in British history. The same pedigree also takes notice of EYNON who was the son of SEILYFF Lord of Canterfellif the son of Griffith Lord of Cwmwdon the son of Ellisser the son of Iscordia Vawr, the son of Iscordia Vychan the son of Ellsey the son of Ellay the son of Rho Lord of Cwmwdon the son of Brycham Lord of Brecknock

The EGYPTIANS (sayth PIERIUS) used to signify by the Rere-Mouse a man that having small means and weak power either of Nobility or of Fortune or yett stored with pregnant Witt hath nevertheless stept up so suddenly that he might seem not so much to be supported by the earth as by a sudden flight to be exalted above it. This small animall doth partake both with bird and beast. in such neerness of resemblance to either of them as that it may with reason be doubted of whether kind it be. By occasion whereof he taketh advantage in the battell between beasts and birds menconed in Æsop to flutter above them to behold the engagement & then strike in to the stronger and conquering side. Of all birds according to Pliny they alone bringeth forth young alive and none but shee hath wings made of pannicles or thin skinns. So shee is the only bird that suckleth her young with her paps and giveth milk. In the Ensignes of the Kingdome of INDIA this bird is born in Pale three of them one above another sorted among the Coat.armors of a multitude of the great assembly holden at the Councel of Constance A.o Dom. 1414. Guil. displ. of Heraldrie, Sect. 3. Chap. 26. pag. 263.

Fragments of Broad Street roofs are shown in the foreground and the Black Swan is labelled, though mistakenly drawn with its gable end facing the schoolhouse. Dineley evidently favoured an impressionistic approach above accuracy.

West House and No. 22 on the south side of Broad Street. Their back rooms together formed one malthouse in Dineley's time. These present frontages were added c.1775

A fragment of gable end that seems to be on the opposite side of Broad Street is probably that of the former malthouse that today forms the back parts of both West House and No. 22. In 1684 it consisted of a rectangular stone structure set ten paces behind the cobbled pavement and sideways on to it. Its huge stone chimney stack, which carried away all the smoke directed under a perforated floor to dry the barley, is still in place.

The most striking thing about Dineley's sketch is the open space between the schoolhouse (formerly St John's Chapel) and the Black Swan. Indeed there is nothing but space all round the schoolhouse; other buildings are

OPPOSITE: A page from Thomas Dineley's notebook of 1684. The circular drawing shows St John's as a schoolroom and the Black Swan (© Hereford Cathedral)

The Castle, from Thomas Dineley, *The Official Progress of the First Duke of Beaufort Through Wales in 1684* (© Hereford Cathedral)

well distant. Chancery Lane and the top half of Brook Street clearly did not yet exist and this part of town appears to have been almost as open as in Norman times.

Dineley made two sketches of Hay, both confined within circular borders, and neither view is attainable from anywhere in town so he presumably crossed the Wye and looked back. Perhaps he used a spyglass from the fields on the other side.

In his second sketch Hay Castle is shown towering above the roofs of Castle Street with the steep ascent up to it made more gradual by obtrusively fenced zigzag paths. The gateway onto Castle Street has ornamental stone pillars almost identical to those of the main entrance on Oxford Road.

Dineley finished his journal entry for Hay with a brief statement on its economy: 'The commodities are cotton, corn, cattle, fish and some otter'. In 1684 the word 'cotton' did not indicate a fibre. It referred to the smooth texture of a fabric, and here Dineley is almost certainly talking about the woollen flannel that had long been manufactured in the town.

Hay had probably had two fulling mills producing flannel since the fourteenth century, when sheep farming in the surrounding areas increased after the Black Death. One hundred and twenty or so years into the future The Granary would be built further down Broad Street, not initially for storing grain as its name suggests, but more probably for storing wool. Today it is a popular café and restaurant.

Dineley's remaining items, fish and otter, were both connected with the River Wye. Salmon and eels were probably the most popular fish in seventeenth-century Hay. Otters were trapped for their fur but would later be brought to the edge of extinction in order to protect the fish and the town's reputation as a fishing centre. They are making a comeback, however, and today the Wye now holds one of the densest and most well-established otter populations in Britain.

The First Bridge, 1763

If Dineley did indeed cross the Wye to make his sketches of Hay he must have used the town ferry – or, if the river was low enough, the ford. There was no bridge at that time. Indeed John Leland had claimed that, in his time, there was no bridge anywhere between Hereford and Builth.[10]

Clyro was just over a mile away, but although it was also in Wales it might almost have been in a foreign country. That side of the Wye was the former land of Elfael, the enemy territory whose youths had dared each other to raid Hay Castle and steal the lord's doves. Now it was called Radnorshire but it was still the least populated county in Wales, the condition of its roads so poor that sledges drawn by horses or oxen were used instead of wheeled vehicles because they ran more easily over ruts and potholes.

Great herds of Welsh Black cattle made their way along the drovers' road through Clyro to the Rhydspence and on to the fattening fields of the English Midlands, but the people of Hay were barely even aware of them. The lowing of cows being herded along drovers' roads could often travel miles over the countryside, but here it was largely blocked by a ridge of high ground. As far as Hay was concerned the Clyro side of this ridge was an alien land, unseen, unheard and largely ignored.

By the middle of the eighteenth century, however, roads everywhere were improving, people were travelling more, and a bridge over the Wye had begun to seem both desirable and financially feasible. Turnpike Trusts were showing that the cost of maintaining roads could be met with tolls, so why should not a bridge be paid for in the same way? All matters of that sort had to go before Parliament and the Hay Bridge Act, empowering commissioners to reimburse the cost of building and maintaining a bridge by the collection of tolls, was passed in 1756.

Hay's first bridge, built by a contractor in return for a lease on the tolls, had five splendid stone arches and was opened in 1763. People could now cross the Wye without risk of getting wet and animals could be taken from Radnorshire to the markets on Broad Street, no matter how high the river rose over the ford.

As a point of access to the bridge on the Hay side, the entryway between the Three Tuns and the Black Swan had been chosen. It was barely wide enough for large horse-drawn farm vehicles to turn into (and has given many a lorry driver a headache in the days since), but was the best place for connecting with the road from Clyro. The remains of the old town wall were removed from its far end and replaced by a toll gate with a toll house close by, and so Bridge Street was created. It was short and steeper than today, the original bridge being 16 feet lower than the present one.

Hay was somewhat less isolated after the bridge was built, but not dramatically so. It was still remote from the main trading routes servicing the Industrial Revolution and so remained essentially the small rural market town it had always been.

The name of Broad Street changed for a time to Wye Bridge Street but otherwise life went on much as before. Almost everything was still locally, even domestically, produced. The street was still home to the town's cattle, sheep and poultry markets, and the mill site still housed the tannery and twin mill wheels; the upper one grinding corn and the lower one turning woollen material into flannel.

The Turnpike Trusts were proving to be something of a mixed blessing, however. It was true that they performed a valuable service in improving and maintaining the roads, but they were largely composed of wealthy landowners who, it was often suspected, were making indecently high profits from them. Resentment over extortionate tolls ran high.

Particular bad feeling was generated by two toll gates positioned within a short distance of each other, one of them across Broad Street between the mill and the pound opposite.[11] This was run by the Breconshire Turnpike

Poplar House at the junction of Broad Street with Heol y Dwr.
The Ebeneezer Congregational Chapel (now The Globe) is in the background

Trust; while the other, run by a Herefordshire trust, was just 300 yards away at the bottom of Newport Street. The cost of getting animals from Clifford to the markets on Broad Street was therefore felt to be unreasonably high. At the Broad Street gate, farmers had to pay ten pence to bring a score of cattle through, and five pence for a score of sheep, when they had already paid something similar at the bottom of the hill. And if they came in a horse and cart it was another threepence at each gate.[12] Sums that sound trivial today then represented significant amounts of money. And it was no good trying to evade the tolls by using a different route for this could occasion hefty fines.

Tredegar House behind the clock tower was once a popular pub called The King's Head

Once through the toll gates and onto Broad Street, there were plenty of alehouses where farmers could complain to each other about the cost of getting there. The Three Tuns, the Black Swan, the Rose and Crown, and the Seven Stars were all on the northern side, and up by the Tump at the bottom of Cranbourne Alley (now the Pavement) was the King's Head. There was another, called the Old White Lion, on the south side but that has now disappeared (*see Chapter 8*).

THE SOUTH SIDE OF BROAD STREET c.1775
Back in 1684, Dineley had shown St John's as a schoolhouse in apparently good repair. Ninety years later, however, in 1774 and 1775, the court rolls for Hay reported that 'a great quantity of stone, being fell from the ruings of St John's church in this Borough are a great nuisance and ought to be from thence removed.'[13] Possibly then it is no coincidence that Prospect House, on the corner of Chancery Lane, was built at that time. Perhaps the stones were carted the few hundred yards from St John's and reused in this large, double-fronted, typically symmetrical Georgian house. In years to come the Stokoe family would live here, as would the Wigingtons. Richard Booth's arch rival, Leon Morelli, would re-christen it Chancery House and commit the sacrilege of putting railings round the raised cobbled pavement at the front.

CHANCERY LANE

Chancery Lane was once known as Pig Lane because pigpens were erected down the length of it on market days. The pig market itself was held at the crossroads by Tomatito's (once The Wheatsheaf) and St John's. The unpaved road surface would be much churned up by the pigs, and since their droppings were rarely cleared away this whole area became 'a great nuisance'. Sir Joseph Bailey (who later created the Bailey Walk along the riverbank), would, in 1873, be requested by the Local Board to flag or pave around the walls of St John's in order to minimise this nuisance.

Chancery Lane cottages in the process of demolition in the 1960s

TOP: The six houses to the east of Pig Lane were all apparently built c.1775.
BOTTOM: No. 25a and Brynhyfryd. No. 25a (the yellow-brick house on the left) was built on the site of Brynhyfryd's former coach house

Chancery Lane was once known as Gravel Lane,[14] which suggests that it may have been gravelled, perhaps until about this time when cottages were built there. The first mention of these dates from 1790. It was also commonly known as Pig Lane.

Down from Prospect House, the former malthouse was now divided in two, its drying room and window on the ground floor sliced through by a thin partition. New rooms and a staircase were added to the larger section to bring the frontage forward and in line with Prospect House. This is now West House.

The remaining third of the malthouse, and the paved area once outside its front door, became the central part of another house, now No. 22. Strangely, given that it shares its origins with West House, it is completely different in style, being taller and thinner. It was paired instead with another of the same type, now No. 21.

Beyond West House, another classically double-fronted Georgian house, now called Sycamore House, was built facing straight down Bridge Street and over the bridge. No definite date for its construction is known but it is also thought to be of *c.*1775.

Beyond that again, Brynhyfryd is non-symmetrical and probably had older origins. It once had a coach house on the site where No. 25a, the tall yellow-brick house, now stands.

By 1841, when the first national census was completed, these six houses were occupied largely by the professional classes: two by surgeons and two by attorneys-at-law. The raised cobbled pavement in front of them would continue to be used by market traders until well into the 1960s, with the right of way immediately in front of the houses preserved.

Further down towards the clock tower, the large double-fronted Bank House, with steps extending from the front door down to the pavement, also seems to have been there by 1778, but it replaced something much older. There are records of a dwelling here in 1596. For many years Bank House would be the home of William Acton, maltster and Mayor of Hay, and subsequently that of the manager of Barclays Bank.

OVERLEAF: *Hay on Wye and the Brecon Beacons* (1846) by Joseph Murray Ince (1806–59). (Image courtesy of the National Library of Wales). Note the hybrid bridge on the right side

A Hybrid Bridge

Hay's first bridge would stay intact for just 32 years, lasting only until February 1795 when the melt water from a severe frost swept away three of its five stone arches. The bridges upstream at Glasbury and downstream at Whitney went at the same time, and it would be two years before Glasbury got its bridge back. Hay bridge was repaired more quickly but the work was done on the cheap. The lease stipulated that stone should be used, but five piers of timber were added to the two stone arches left on the far side, making a kind of hybrid structure.

It would last longer than its predecessor in spite of this, although by 1838 the *Hereford Times* was describing it as being in a very dilapidated state. It would not be replaced until the railway arrived in 1864.

4

Two Railways, The Crown and the Clock Tower

James Spencer and the Hay Railway

Between Bank House and the corner of Chancery Lane is an old building with huge oak beams, that today is called The Boardroom. Until comparatively recently it was open from the ground floor to the roof and at one time the door fittings were reputedly Elizabethan. The building may well date from that time.

Known today as The Boardroom, this was probably James Spencer's office for much of his career as a Hay solicitor

In the early 1800s, however, it was the office of a solicitor called James Spencer. He worked hard to ensure that Hay's first so-called railway was completed, yet he has rarely been given the credit for it, perhaps because he ended his life in gaol. It is a strange but true fact about Broad Street that two of its solicitors have died in prison. The other, 70 years later, would be Herbert Rowse Armstrong. Hay historian, Geoffrey Fairs, puts them both into his 'Rogues Gallery'[1] but in each case (though for different reasons) it can be argued that this is less than fair.

James Spencer's career began promisingly. He was born in Ireland in 1770, and by 1811 had an extensive portfolio of properties and farming interests in the Hay area. He lived on the other side of the river at Lower Cabalva but also owned Bank House on Broad Street, the building at the far end of town that would become the Hay workhouse, and much else besides. He would later live at No. 22 Broad Street, so he probably owned that as well, and at some point he seems to have also acquired the building that is now Gabb & Co at the bottom of Chancery Lane. All the papers from his long working life were stored in the attic there after his death.

The Hay Railway was in reality a tramway, or wagonway, for at the beginning of the nineteenth century there were no railways as such. Brunel would not succeed in engineering a track from Stockton to Darlington, to create the first steam railway in the world, until 1816.

The idea for the Hay Railway came from a group composed largely of coalmine owners (then called ironmasters) from South Wales, who were looking for ways to extend the market for their coal northwards into Herefordshire. They held their meetings at the Swan Inn, Hay, halfway between the intended end points of Brecon and Eardisley, and conveniently close to James Spencer's office. For although at first he attended purely to give legal advice, it would not be long before he was carrying virtually the whole administrative burden of the project.

If coal went inland at all at that time it was either by road or canal. The group looked at the possibility of building a canal up to Hay but soon discarded that idea in favour of a more innovative plan. They would lay rails along a 24-mile route from the Brecon and Abergavenny Canal to Eardisley and lease them out to contractors, who would then use horses to draw coal wagons along them.

Coal wagons, or trams, were normally used only within the mines, running on rails from the coal face to the point where the coal could be taken up to the surface. Just occasionally, however, and only where the geography was suitable, the rails were extended out of the mine and the trams ran down to the nearest port or waterway under the action of gravity. Horses would then pull them back up to the mines once they were empty. The idea of using horses to pull laden wagons was relatively new, and fraught with difficulty. Gradients would have to be carefully calculated and controlled along the whole route. Major engineering works would be called for.

It was a plan that appealed to proprietors of the Turnpike Trusts, for the transportation of coal along their roads was causing extensive damage. When Spencer drew up the bill that was to go before Parliament he worded it with this in mind:

> Whereas the Turnpike Roads in the Neighbourhood of the Town of Hay, in the County of Brecon, have been greatly injured and destroyed by Carriages travelling thereon, laden with Coals, Corn and other heavy Commodities, which are carried to and from the Brecknock and Abergavenny Canal and the adjoining Counties of Hereford and Radnor, and owing to the constant Draught of such heavy Commodities thereon, are now in a very dilapidated and ruinous state and cannot be kept in repair, even at enormous Expense.[2]

The 'very dilapidated and ruinous state' of the roads being a matter of universal concern, the project won the support of just about everyone of consequence in the area, including seven MPs. Parliament approved the bill, and the Act incorporating the proprietors of the proposed railway under the style of 'The Hay Railway Company' received Royal Assent from George III on 25 May 1811.[3]

And now Spencer's labours really began. The list of his responsibilities was endless. He advised the landowners over whose land the line was to be taken, and had the land valued and purchased. He invited tenders, advertised for contractors and staff, gathered statistics, prepared estimates, and wrote dozens of official letters. Once construction of the tramroad was underway, he organised haulage of the tramplates from Talgarth to

Hay, found land to store them on and paid £60 for that storage, to be later reimbursed by the committee. When a contractor withdrew his labour it was Spencer who was instructed to 'obtain possession of the work.' He was acting as clerk of the works, quantity surveyor and legal executive all rolled into one.

But his greatest headache came in getting the Company's 107 named subscribers to pay up when their subscriptions became due. Ironmaster Sir Charles Morgan, Bart, MP, was among the most reluctant to pay – although he was, ironically, one of those who had initiated the project. When he defaulted on the second call, Spencer wrote to him on 2 June 1812:

> By the Hay Railway Treasurer's Book you stand in arrears for the last call of 10% due 6th January, which it would be pleasant to have paid within the month of June ... I am writing to every subscriber in arrears of which there seem a great many and hope to get most of the money in before the next meeting which is fixed for 3rd July.[4]

His hopes were not realised. A great many subscribers allowed their arrears to remain unpaid in spite of numerous reminders, until finally Spencer was instructed by the Committee to institute legal proceedings against them. And still the company remained chronically short of money.

Sir Charles Morgan, MP for Brecon and then for Monmouthshire, was described by one of his Parliamentary opponents as a 'handsome little man ... possessed of great power', and he was certainly wealthy. He could have paid his subscriptions without batting an eyelid, yet he made Spencer apply to him twice, or even three times, on every call.

For his part, however, Spencer was determined that the project would reach completion. To prevent its collapse he not only allowed his salary to go unpaid for years but used large sums of his own money to meet the bills that were flooding in. Money that the company was reluctant to repay. By December 1821, five years after the railway had reached Hay, he was still owed so much that the interest alone amounted to £634 16s.

The first section of the tramway ended at Hay and was opened on 14 May 1816. It ran from a junction with the Brecon and Abergavenny Canal in Brecon and passed through Talgarth, Porthamal, Glasbury, Llanigon and

Sheep House before making a deep curve across the Warren,[5] just outside Hay. From there it was carried on a terrace cut into the side of the riverbank at an increasing height until it reached the level of Hay bridge; a long, slow haul for the horses. That terrace is still faintly visible today in one or two places, although overgrown with vegetation. Most of it has eroded away.

The track passed over Bridge Street on a level crossing. And from there it went on to cross the Dulais Brook on a bridge specially built for it a few feet from the road. That bridge is still there today, hung heavily with creepers. The line ended at a coal wharf on the far side of the Dulais, the word 'wharf' betraying the way in which this early, horse-drawn railway was seen as an extension of the canal system.

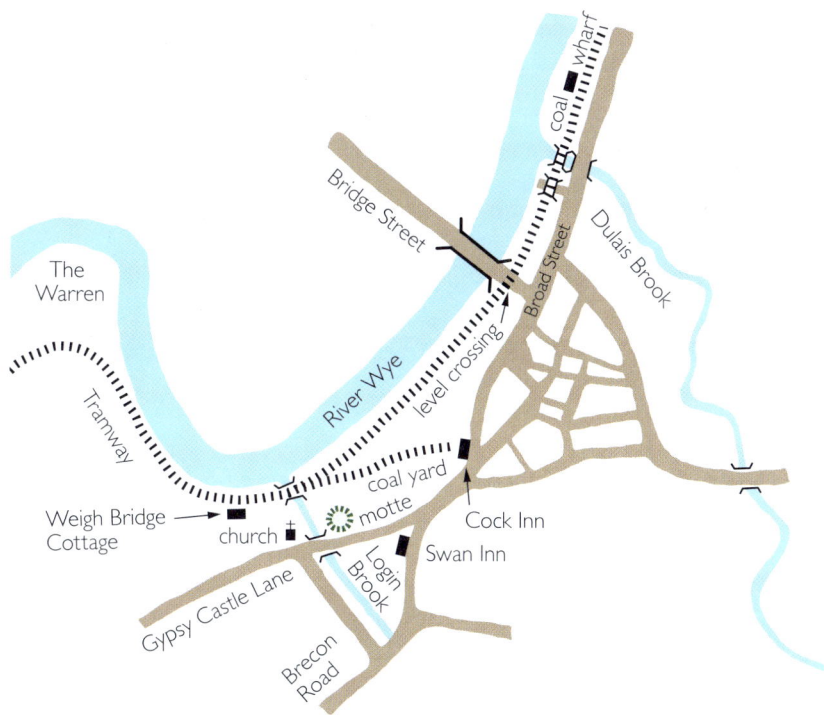

Map of the tramway route through Hay

Two years later the line was taken on to Eardisley and when it joined with the Kington Railway in 1820 it became, at 36 miles, the longest railway in the world. It would continue to hold that title until 1837.

The wharf by the Dulais was too far out of town to be the main point of access for the sale of coal, however. Most of it was therefore taken up a branch line to the old motte and bailey castle (now the cattle market), which became the main coal yard. Its office was in the old Cock Inn, later the Wye Hotel and now Jones Home Hardware. Some of the rails from this branch line were later reused as fence posts that are still in place today.

Tramway rails later used as fence posts near the route of the branch line

Once the wagons had been unloaded at the Cock Wharf they were allowed to run back down to the junction unsupervised under the force of gravity. Unsupervised, that is, until an old woman was killed. She was crossing the line on a path that led to the churchyard when she was struck on the head by the first of two trucks and run over by the second, dying instantaneously. The railway company was severely censored by the coroner for allowing so dangerous a practice.[6]

Most country people were using wood for fuel at the start of the nineteenth century, and many would continue to do so. It threw out less heat than coal but it was cheaper, sometimes even freely available, and did not leave a layer of soot on the furniture. The arrival of coal in Hay did not, therefore, guarantee a ready market for it. The price had to be right, and the coal had to be easily accessible. A second coal market was therefore established near the King's Head at the bottom of Cranbourne Alley (now the Pavement) for the convenience of the farmers who frequented Broad Street on market days. That triangle of road, now usually referred to as 'by the clock tower' would be known as the Coal Market for many years to come.

By 1841 Spencer was 70 and should probably have retired, for he was beginning to lose his grip. Much of his former wealth had already slipped through his fingers, and the national census of that year records him as living, not at Lower Cabalva, but in the far more modest No. 22 Broad Street. He would continue as Solicitor and Clerk to the Hay Railway Company for another five years, though by this time his duties were minimal. The bulk of the work had been passed to others.

By living on Broad Street, however, he was on hand to witness a major event in the life of the town, made possible to a large extent by his own hard work and tenacity, for in 1841 the streets of Hay were lit up at night for the first time in history.

The Hay gas works had been built the year before by the Hay Gas and Coke Company, formed of local landowners and tradespeople under the leadership of Hay's vicar, the Revd Humphrey Allen. There would be hundreds of these small companies all across the UK in the years to come, but Hay was in the forefront of the trend at that time. The steady supply of coal brought in by the tramway had given it the edge.

The Revd Humphrey Allen had made a low-lying piece of land available at the bottom of Newport Street, between Wyeford Road and the Dulais Brook, and within a year of the works opening the company was ready to provide the town with gas street lighting. A large crowd of people met at the Rose and Crown on Broad Street to celebrate the occasion, and after a few drinks they marched through the town headed by a band and a lamplighter. Each newly installed street light was ceremonially lit and each in turn was toasted, beginning with those on Broad Street. Few present on that occasion had seen anything like it. Hay's gas-lit streets were a marvel to behold.

After this triumph, however, Spencer's life went ever more steeply downhill. He was declared bankrupt in 1842 but struggled on, trying to keep his head above water, until the crunch point came in 1847 when he was arrested for debt and incarcerated.

A photograph of the Hay Gas Works taken in the second half of the nineteenth century. Only a single gas holder was needed while gas was used solely for lighting, but here there are two. (Note the bracket for the gas light on the wall on the right)

The debt in question dated from right back in 1813 when he had been asked to invest £600 at 5% per annum on behalf of the Gwynn's Almshouse charity. For 27 years after that he had passed over the yearly interest of £30 and nobody thought to enquire where the £600 capital had gone. Charities were not tightly regulated at that time. By 1847, however, he was no longer in a position to pay the £30 yearly interest. Questions were asked, and he eventually received a court order demanding that he give back the original £600, plus a year's interest of £30, and another £2 10s on top of that. It was a total of £632 10s and he had no means of paying it.

Geoffrey Fairs assumes that Spencer took the £600 for himself. A more likely explanation, however, is that he had invested it in the Hay Railway. He had been having great trouble getting subscribers to pay their dues in 1813, and it had no doubt seemed to him like a good long-term investment.

A c.1862 lithograph by J. Newman & Co. showing a distant view of Hay from the west. Just discernible below the church on the right-hand side is the horse-drawn tram (circled)

He firmly believed that the railway would ultimately make a profit. The interest of £30 a year he so scrupulously paid for 27 years must have come out of his own pocket, as had so much else pertaining to the railway. His biggest failing seems to have been an inability to hold onto his own money.

James Spencer spent the last four years of his life in Hereford Gaol, dying there at the age of 80, a broken and embittered old man. He had never married and in his will he left the remnants of his estate to his faithful housekeeper. His death certificate records that he died by 'a Visitation of God', which today would be given as 'natural causes'. He had given up hope.

His solicitor's practice was eventually taken over by R. Trevor Griffiths who expanded it and moved into the building in Chancery Lane that is now Gabb & Co. Spencer's office was used for board meetings by Trevor Griffiths and thus became known as The Boardroom. A mass of paperwork left from Spencer's time, including the Minutes Book of the Hay Railway Company's meetings at the Swan Inn, eventually found its way to HARC (the Hereford Archive and Records Centre), where the material can be consulted by request.

Sir Charles Morgan made a huge fortune from Welsh coal. As industrial revolutions gathered pace in other parts of the world, the demand for high quality, relatively smokeless Welsh coal soared and a black tide of it flowed out from the ports of South Wales. He died in 1846 aged 86, having bought the Swan Inn and rebuilt it, in 1821, as the Swan Hotel that stands today.

The tramway lasted until the steam railway was brought through in 1864. It had made a modest profit for 40 years.

Thomas Savin and the Hereford, Hay and Brecon Railway Company, 1864

Hay may have been one of the first places in the country to have street lighting, courtesy of the early Hay Railway, but steam trains were late in arriving.

The first inter-city railway in the world had opened in 1830, running from London to Liverpool, and since trains were faster and cheaper than stagecoaches the country was soon in the grip of railway mania. By the 1840s the rail network was spreading over most of England, and by 1850 there were lines along the coasts of north and south Wales. But the central part of Wales remained virtually untouched. Here the population was so sparse that it proved impossible to raise enough share subscriptions. Few believed that a railway across mid Wales could make a profit.

Gradually, though, that began to change. As companies continued to look for the easiest and most potentially lucrative routes, the idea began to seem more feasible. Several proposals were made, and dropped; several companies dissolved before anything practical had been achieved. But the Hereford, Hay and Brecon Railway Company was one that did manage to last until its railway was operational. It encountered many difficulties along the way but managed to weather them, largely because it had been fortunate enough to secure the services of a contractor called Thomas Savin.

By 1861 the HH&BR had entered negotiations for the purchase of the Hay Railway (tramway). It was still functioning at that time and represented a valuable potential asset to a steam railway company, its route being ready-engineered. All that was needed, along most of its length, was conversion from narrow to standard gauge and it would be fit to carry steam trains. Two other companies were also interested, but since each wanted a different section of the line, agreement was reached fairly readily. The three companies would buy the Hay Railway jointly, then divide it up between them. All that remained for the HH&BR was to decide how it was going to pay for its share of the purchase price.

Meetings were held and much wrangling ensued. Railway companies were notorious for the squabbling that took place amongst their committee members. But Thomas Savin, waiting to get started on the construction work, was impatient. He was keen to get the job done and move on. Eventually then, when he could stand it no longer, he cut through the argumentation by putting up all the money himself and accepting company shares in return. He was now a shareholder.

But there was a further and even greater difficulty. The level-crossing at the bottom of Bridge Street had been safe enough with slow horse-drawn wagons, but it was a dangerous proposition when it came to steam trains. Especially as Bridge Street was quite short and sloped steeply down towards it. The Board of Trade were adamant that continued use of the level-crossing was not to be thought of.

The alternative was that trains should pass under Bridge Street, or in effect the bridge itself as it extended over the river bank. But the problem here was that the line could not be taken low enough for the trains to pass under without becoming flooded when river levels rose in winter.

Much further discussion ensued and various ideas were put forward, including that of taking the railway on a different route altogether around the other side of town. But Savin listened to it all with mounting impatience. To him the answer was clear. Hay bridge should be rebuilt at a higher level so that trains could pass underneath.

The *Hereford Times* would later describe the Hay bridge of this time as 'a crazy old structure, spliced, propped and patched in all directions, with dangerous approaches on each side' (29 April 1865). But it was not nearly as evident to everyone else as it was to Savin that the bridge was therefore in need of replacement. On the contrary. The timber part had been completely replaced after several weeks of hard frost had given way to a sudden thaw in 1855, and masses of floating ice had crashed into it, breaking it apart. By 1863 therefore the new timber section had been in place for only eight years.

So the wrangling continued and Savin became increasingly frustrated. He was in a hurry to get back to a project on the Welsh coast that was dear to his heart. A railway station was due to open in Aberystwyth the following year and he was spending £80,000 to build a hotel nearby. It was a large sum, but he was gambling on people taking seaside holidays in Aberystwyth once they could get there by train. How to encourage them to stay at his hotel rather than anywhere else? He had a plan for that. Passengers on Welsh railways would be able to buy tickets that included the cost of accommodation at his Castle Hotel. It was, probably, the world's first package deal.

Back in Hay then he stood up at one of the endless meetings and proposed to bear the cost of building a new bridge across the Wye himself. It would be 16 feet higher than the existing one so that trains could pass underneath. And he was willing to take in exchange, he said, a 99-year lease on the tolls. His offer was immediately accepted.

So a new bridge was built, and it was completely different to anything that had gone before. All the stone and wood were swept away and in their place rose a tall, elegant structure of cast iron with lattice girders and ladder-like splayed piers.

Hay Bridge.

A postcard view of Savin's delicate, wrought-iron bridge

A photograph of c.1950 showing Hay station, with Savin's bridge beyond

Once Savin had rebuilt Hay Bridge 16 feet higher, trains could pass underneath.
The bank on which the boys are sitting is now wooded

A problem for the future would be that the weight limit of the new bridge was only five tons and this would be reduced even further over the coming years as motorised transport increased. By the 1950s it was only two and a half tons. There are those who still remember coming to Hay by bus on market days and having to get off on the far side of the river because Savin's beautiful bridge was not strong enough to bear the weight of the bus. It would be completely replaced in 1957.

Back in 1864, however, the new bridge was a triumph. Trains could pass underneath and Bridge Street had been made less formidably steep into the bargain. Hay Station was on the far side of the Dulais Brook, where the coal wharf for the tramway had been, and the first passenger train pulled into it on 24 September, 1864. The Hay and Hereford Rifle Corps Band led a procession up Newport Street to a magnificent lunch at the Rose and Crown on Broad Street. And a monster picnic behind the Nelson Inn on Newport Street (now Kingfisher House) catered for 2,000 people – more than the entire population of the town.

Trains were not only faster than horse-drawn vehicles, they were cheaper. Conversations like the following were soon to be heard everywhere:

> Wonders will never cease, you see. Here we be in this carriage, which is a very nice one only the windows be dirty, and for 1/9d it will take us to Hay and back. In the old coach they charged us 10/- and we was travelling all day nearly.[7]

Thomas Savin meanwhile was over-extending himself financially. By 1866 his various enterprises were worth well over £1 million but when his bank, the Overend Gurney, failed in that year their value dropped overnight. He was just 40 years of age, and bankrupt. The Aberystwyth hotel on which he had spent in excess of £80,000 was sold for a mere £10,000.

But he weathered the storm. He pulled out of railways and hotels and, retaining only the ownership of a limestone quarry, turned his attention to local politics and gardening. He would go on to become mayor of his home town of Oswestry in Shropshire and a Fellow of the Royal Horticultural Society.

Kilvert's Diary

Six months after the railway was completed in 1864, a young man arrived by train at Hay station. He was heading for Clyro (just north-west of Hay), where he had obtained a post as curate, and the diary he would begin to keep five years later would become a minor classic. Some of its most poignant passages are set in and around Clyro, an area now sometimes referred to as Kilvert Country.

Francis Kilvert's life in Clyro would concentrate mainly on his parishioners, many of whom lived in isolated farmsteads, and for many of whom he felt a real affection. Their way of life had remained unchanged for generations and he was deeply appreciative of the continuity. Here was a backwater remote from the breakneck speed of change in Victorian England where people were deserting the land in droves. There may have been pockets of abject poverty, but life was at least stable.

He was less enamoured with Hay. Of the Hay Fairs he wrote how glad he was to be away from 'the noise, bustle, dust, drunkenness, and the general upturn of the country.' He describes how 'squadrons of horse came charging and battalions of foot tramping along the dusty roads' to the great May Hiring Fair and of how he saw plough boys going to the town in droves to hire.

The *Hereford Times* of 17 June 1865 took a similar view:

> the streets of the town rendered impassable by droves of white-faced Herefords, sheep and horses. Along the turnpike roads or paths through the fields might have been seen little batches of Welsh people bound for Hay, the old men invariably with their coats slung loosely over their shoulders, the women arrayed in their gayest attire, with their delicate little hands encased in gloves ... Pity them having to climb the stiles with crinolines ...

From time to time, however, Kilvert did walk the mile-and-a-half into town. He would have been a familiar sight on Broad Street with his black eyes and patriarchal beard, the latter so long and heavy it would freeze to his mackintosh on frosty mornings.

> I walked to Hay to pay some bills. On the crest of the hill above Hay I met a tall woman smoking a clay pipe and driving a black donkey. A raven sailed down croaking hoarsely from the hills to the Wye side meadows.
>
> 29 July 1871

If he wasn't paying bills or shopping, Kilvert's destination would often be Hay Castle, occupied at that time by the Revd William Latham Bevan and his family. His wife would offer Kilvert a warm welcome and his daughter was a close friend of the girl Kilvert was in love with, Daisy Thomas. There was always the chance that he would meet her there.

But it was soon made clear to Kilvert that he had no chance of marrying Daisy. He was of the right social class, being a clergyman, but only as a kind of poor relation. His income as a curate was only £100 a year and nowhere near enough to keep a wife in the style to which she would have been accustomed. He would fall in love with other girls once he had given up hope of Daisy, but marriage had to remain out of the question until he could obtain a living.

Like Wordsworth, whom he much admired, Kilvert was essentially a solitary who loved roaming the countryside. To him Hay was a place full of public houses, clubs and Nonconformist chapels, and he had no time for any of them.

> I had a notice asking me to attend a meeting at Hay this afternoon organized to discuss a proposed Club and reading room in Hay, where members can if they like have luncheon, mutton chops. Great nonsense. I did not go.
>
> 7 October 1870

He was especially ready to believe the worst of Nonconformists, whom he called dissenters.

> Some barbarian – a dissenter no doubt – probably a Baptist, has cut down the beautiful silver birches on the Little Mountain.
>
> 18 July 1871

In 1845 Congregationalists had built the Ebeneezer Chapel (now The Globe) on the corner of Broad Street and Heol y Dwr, with a grand entrance high on a grassy bank. The Baptists had an ancient chapel on Bell Bank, and there were chapels for Calvinists, Wesleyan Methodists and Primitive Methodists. The only religious building in the centre of town, where Kilvert might once have felt comfortable, many years before, was St John's Chapel, but that had gone from being a schoolhouse in Dineley's time to becoming a lock-up in 1810.

Kilvert did eventually get a living of his own and was briefly vicar of St Harmons in remote rural Radnorshire before moving to Bredwardine in the Wye Valley. It enabled him to get married at last, at the age of 38, though not to Daisy Thomas. She would never marry. Nor to any of the other young women who appear in his diary. But to a woman called Elizabeth about whom the diary tells us nothing. After his death she would burn some of it, presumably those pages on which she had been mentioned.

Kilvert died of peritonitis within a few days of returning from his honeymoon in 1879 and is buried in Bredwardine churchyard. His grave is marked by a plain white cross on a three-tier plinth inscribed 'In death he yet speaks' – a fitting epitaph for a famous diarist.

The Cheese Brothers and the Crown Hotel, early 1800s

Accidents with horses were common in Kilvert's time. His diary records at least two in Hay, one of them involving Daisy's brother, Major Thomas:

> Then we went to Hay Castle and as we walked up the street we heard a loud sudden crash behind. Major Thomas's horse had shied and bolted into the Rose and Crown Stables. The wheel had caught the post and they were all in a heap together on the ground. Neither the Major nor his servant were hurt, the shafts of the dogcart were smashed and the horse lay on the stones of the gateway like dead till he was freed and then started up almost unhurt and trembling like a leaf, bleeding from the mouth and a scratch on one knee.
>
> 16 September 1871

The Rose and Crown was then twice the length it is today and, like the Swan Inn at the far end of town, was a major stopping place for post horses and stage coaches. Major Thomas had no doubt been heading for the livery stables behind the part that was about to be replaced by the Crown Hotel (now Y Gelli Chambers and the Old Electric Shop).

The livery stables were housed in a long building that stretched halfway down the length of the old burgage plot, and by 1891 were being run by a certain William Colley, who lived in accommodation above the stables with his wife and son, together with two young grooms. Horses could be hired there, but mainly it was a place where owners could keep their horses and have them looked after for a weekly fee. A field on the other side of the Wye provided grazing.

Hay historian David Bennett, who sadly died in 2020, suggests that Thomas Savin owned the Rose and Crown at one time[8] and if so he may well have acquired it with the idea of rebuilding it as a hotel, much as he had done with the Castle Hotel in Aberystwyth. There, he was expecting people to come by train for seaside holidays. In Hay, he would no doubt have been expecting them to come for the Black Mountains scenery and the fishing.

The Wye was said to be the best salmon-fishing river south of Scotland and in 1866 the landlord of the (double-length) Rose and Crown, George Hope, was promoting it by advertising the local fishing opportunities:

> SEVEN MILES OF EXCELLENT AND STRICTLY PRESERVED FISHING IN THE WYE together with several miles of BROOK FISHING. The Hotel is situated too within 30 minutes ride, by rail, of the famous and extensive LLANGORSE LAKE, which abounds in PERCH AND PIKE. Terms exceedingly moderate.[9]

Great tragedy would come upon the Hope family. George had been full of enthusiasm at the time of this advertisement. Four years into the job, he was still only 26. A year later, however, he and his wife, Ann, would lose an 11-month-old son and George himself would be dead before 1871. Ann, who briefly took over from him as landlady of the Rose and Crown, died of consumption soon afterwards.

Drawing by the Hereford firm of J.C. Haddon, architects, showing the Crown Hotel and the proposed changes to the Rose and Crown in the same style. Dated 1879, a pencilled note in the top left-hand corner says 'The Crown Hotel and other property at Hay belonging to Arthur Cheese.' (Photo courtesy of William Beales & Co.)

The idea of rebuilding the Rose and Crown as a large, modern hotel may or may not have come from Thomas Savin but it was eventually taken up by Arthur Cheese, the solicitor who practised in the offices next door. An architect's drawing of the proposed alterations, by Haddon Bros of Hereford, hangs today in his former offices, now occupied by Williams Beales & Co.

In 1879, when these drawings were done, Arthur Cheese was living in London and practising from prestigious premises at No. 40 Chancery Lane. He had handed over the Hay practice to his brother, Edmund Hall Cheese, but continued to own the building that housed its office, together with the Rose and Crown and several other premises on Broad Street. The two brothers no doubt discussed between them the proposed alterations to the Rose and Crown, and it seems from the drawings that their plan was to rebuild half of the Rose and Crown as the Crown Hotel, then have the frontage of the remaining part re-done in the same style. In the event the first part of the plan would come to maturity, but not the second.

The Rose and Crown was a popular hostelry; the venue of choice for the meetings of several societies and numerous club dinners. A vet was on hand there on market days for farmers to consult. But it was the billiard room that was regarded as no less than a local essential, so, since it was in the part due for demolition, Edmund Hall Cheese devised a remedy. He had a billiard table installed on the first floor of his offices and a doorway knocked through to the remaining part of the Rose and Crown. His legal cogitations thereafter were no doubt accompanied by the soft click of billiard balls.

Broad Street in 1920. The low white building on the right is the Rose and Crown with Edmund Cheese's offices adjacent to it in the foreground. These would subsequently become the offices of Herbert Rowse Armstrong (Chapter 6)

It was fortunate that he had had the space to spare. But at some stage a driftway, or passageway, on the far side had been built over and his offices extended. This extension is now occupied by the Yorkshire Building Society and numbered 9a Broad Street.

The Rose and Crown had been built in the seventeenth century, and the Cheese brothers' new hotel was completely different in style. Out of keeping, it might be said, with the rest of the street, although inside it was splendid. Completed in 1880 or thereabouts, it had bedrooms for 12 guests with seven more for live-in staff. There were several sitting rooms and a large dining room on the ground floor. It would cease to be a hotel in the 1990s, but the name remains set into the pavement in front of the main entrance in brass letters.

By 1883 Arthur Cheese had acquired all the property on this side of Broad Street from the Crown Hotel down to, and including, No. 6. In his booklet on Hay pubs[10] David Bennett wrote, '1883 – I have a document and although undated I am sure it links in to other documents for this year'. Apparently in connection with properties owned by Arthur Cheese this gives:

The Crown Hotel with the Rose and Crown as they are today.
The plan to have them both in the same style was never realised

Purchase of Rose and Crown	£1,300. 0. 0
For fixtures as per W Sunderlands valuation	97. 11. 0
Contract for new additions to Crown Hotel	1,825. 0. 0
Alterations and repairs to old part of house	100. 0. 0
Architect's fee	100. 0. 0
Gas fitter	44. 4. 3
Purchase of house No. 9 Broad St (now 9b) with billiard room adjoining the Crown Hotel	630. 0. 0
Purchase of	
— a Grocer's shop with garden and outbuilding in the occupation of Edwin Browning. (No. 6)	
— a house adjoining, late in the occupation of John Baker, but now vacant (No. 8) and	
— a dwelling-house, now occupied as offices by Messrs Cheese, all Broad Street	600. 0. 0

Arthur Cheese died shortly after this. His brother, Edmund Hall Cheese, inherited the Crown Hotel but soon sold it, apparently to his former clerk, Richard Littlewood. The bill of sale, dated 22 July 1884, makes clear that the Crown Hotel, the Rose and Crown, the stables, coach houses and gardens, together with 'the flat then used as a billiard room on first floor of the office of E.H. Cheese' all went for £1,700. It was less than the project had cost. The Cheese brothers had lost out on the gamble of building a grand hotel, as Thomas Savin had done before them.

Edmund Hall Cheese would continue as a Broad Street solicitor for many years. He was Clerk to the Hay Magistrates, but also played an active role in the wider community. He and Arthur were both supporters of the short-lived Golden Valley Railway, and as Capt. Edmund Hall Cheese he was commander of the Breconshire (1st) Volunteer Battalion, South Wales Borderers, based at the Drill Hall in Lion Street.

He would acquire a partner as he grew older, and his solicitor's practice would become Cheese and Armstrong. Herbert Rowse Armstrong would take over from him as captain of the Drill Hall volunteers, and as Clerk to the Hay Magistrates. But he would be dead by the time Armstrong's name hit the headlines of the national newspapers.

The Broad Street Tump and the Clock Tower, 1884

A few yards up from the Crown Hotel is a triangle of road that joins Broad Street to Belmont Road, the Pavement and Lion Street.

The clock tower stands there today and the area is generally referred to as 'by the clock tower'. In the past, however, it had other names. When the tramway was operating it was known as the Coal Market, though its more enduring name was The Square. This was the town's main market square for centuries and the place where large open-air gatherings were held. The Wye Valley Hunt still meets there every Boxing Day, although most other events are now held in the Memorial Square in front of the castle.

But that Broad Street triangle of road was also apparently once known as The Tump. In 1907 C.G. Portman wrote:

> Until a few years ago the square, where the Town clock stands, was called 'The Tump', and the present vicarage is built on the site of an old house

called 'The Tump House', which was surrounded with fir trees (the writer's grandmother has often spoken of these trees) and at the present day one is still standing on the lawn.[11]

Tump House and the Tump itself would have been familiar sights to James Spencer, though Tump House was demolished just before he was imprisoned in 1847, for a land agent called Charles Griffiths had plans to erect a new and more modern dwelling in its place. This would be a three-storey affair with bay windows, set back from the road but facing down the length of Broad Street The house would be called Belle Vue, perhaps because of this, though the central object in the view at that time was the tollgate at Pound Head. Charles Griffiths was much involved with various Turnpike Trusts and Highway Boards.[12]

Once Belle Vue was completed, Broad Street had a commanding new building at either end, each built within five years of the other. Charles Griffith's house was at one end and the Ebeneezer Chapel (now The Globe) was at the other. Kilvert would doubtless have known both.

Of the Tump itself, however, little is known. Though the fact that it was there no doubt explains why neither the Pavement nor Lion Street extend as far as the line of Broad Street. It may have been a dung heap, or possibly some kind of prehistoric tumulus. On Guy Fawkes Night 1850, a crowd gathered round it to watch and rejoice as effigies of the Pope and Cardinal Wiseman were burned. An injudiciously worded letter, written by the cardinal, had led them into the mistaken belief that the Pope was trying to seize temporal power in Britain.[13]

Belle Vue, built by Charles Griffiths in the late 1840s, would later become the vicarage for St Mary's and then for many years the Council Offices

A print of 1814 showing the bottom of Cranbourne Alley (The Pavement)

Detail of the clock tower

The decision to replace the Tump with a clock tower was made around 1881. Before the railway era each part of the country had kept its own time, making it virtually impossible to co-ordinate train timetables, and necessitating the introduction of something called railway time. Many Welsh towns, including Knighton in Radnorshire, had erected a tall, stand-alone clock tower in a prominent place so that railway time could be clearly seen. By the time Hay's tower was operational, however, Greenwich Mean Time had become the legally standardised time across Britain.

Once the decision had been made, however, considerable efforts were needed to raise the £600 needed for Hay's clock tower. The Revd Bevan promoted a bazaar that realised £270, and much of the rest came from subscriptions. It was designed by Haddon Bros of Hereford, as the Crown Hotel had been. Though the commission can hardly have been an onerous one, for it would turn out to be almost identical to Knighton's, built 12 years earlier in a style that has been somewhat disparagingly described as 'off the peg Gothic',[13] though it has an interesting structure and much detail.

Hay's tower was almost 50 feet high on completion. It had a small door in the base to give access to the workings of the clock, and a bell that sounded the quarter-hours. The clock was set going at Christmas 1884 and from then on the bell would sound out every quarter of an hour, day and night.

If this irritated the Hincks family who had recently moved into Tinto House they have left no record of the fact, but then they were becoming accustomed to nuisance. The house next door, No. 14, had burned down earlier that year and they were having to suffer the noise and dust of its rebuilding. Thomas Samuel Hawkesford Hincks was a doctor, and when

Tinto House with No. 14 immediately beyond. The white house beyond that again is No. 1 Belmont Road, occupied by Fred Davies, the chemist, and his wife, who played such a significant part in the Armstrong case (*Chapter 6*)

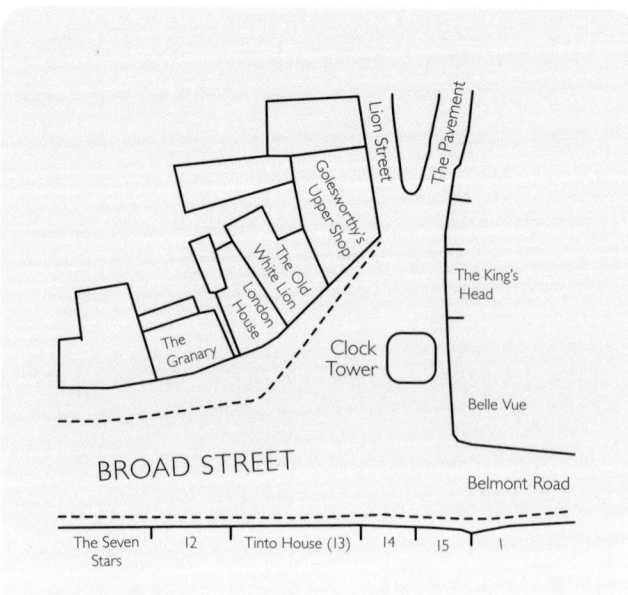

The area at the western end of Broad Street variously known over the years as 'The Tump', 'The Coal Market' and 'The Square'

the clock was set going in 1884, he and his wife, Emily, had four sons aged eight and under, with two young, live-in female servants to cook and do the housework. The eldest of the boys, Thomas Ernest, would himself become a doctor and go into practice with his father, the two of them becoming well-known throughout the district as reliable family doctors. Dr T.E. Hincks would be involved with the Armstrong affair of the early 1920s, and the ground floor of No. 14 would become his surgery.

By 1891 a family called Golesworthy were living opposite to the Hincks on the other side of The Square. The census of that year shows them as having seven children: five girls and two boys, aged between four months and 11 years, with two live-in girl servants, both aged 18, to help look after them all.

Frank Woodland Golesworthy – clothier, outfitter and boot factor – had been born near Honiton in Devon, while his wife, Caroline, came from Dorstone in the Golden Valley. The first Golesworthy shop had opened in Cheltenham in 1877, but since the Hay air was felt to be better for Caroline's health, Frank Woodland had gone on to open a branch on Broad Street. To begin with it occupied just the top third of their present shop, previously a sewing factory.

82   FINDING HAY — A JOURNEY UP BROAD STREET

Golesworthy's first shop, on the corner of Broad Street and Lion Street

Today, Golesworthy's is run by Frank Woodland's great-grandson, Robert, and is nearly three times larger than it was then, selling a wide range of clothing, shoes, maps and accessories for walkers. In addition to the stock, however, it has, in its middle section, a flight of stone steps leading down to a large cellar. A stone flange either side of the steps indicates the means by which beer barrels were once laid across and rolled down. For this is almost certainly the remnant of a former public house called the Old White Lion. If so, it would have been one of four 'lion' pubs in Hay. The others were the White Lion and the Red Lion, both of which were in Lion Street, and the Old Black Lion, now the only one remaining.

The Old White Lion is only known to have existed from a single directory entry of 1835, which gives the landlord's name as Pitt.[14] The plan from 1859 (*overleaf*) shows the premises as a private dwelling, but the note across the top records that it was once in the possession of a certain Henry Pitt, which lends support to the notion that this was once the Old White Lion. The passageway marked as a Right of Way shows that there was once access from the road to what would no doubt have been the stableyard at the back. The night soil also would have been taken out along this passage. Extracted from the cesspit at the back, it would have been sold to local farmers as fertiliser.

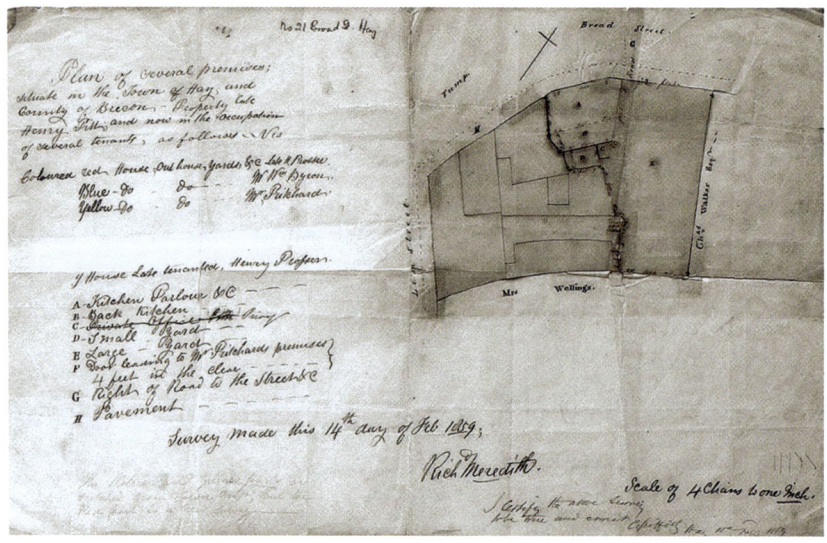

A plan from 1859 shows the position of the Tump. The rooms marked 'A' and 'B' would have been part of the Old White Lion. 'G' shows the right of way through from the road to the yard at the back, now built over as London House.
(Plan courtesy of Robert Golesworthy)

Broad Street on market day pre-1919 when the cattle market was moved to its present site

Today that former passageway is occupied by London House (now part of Golesworthy's) which, like No. 25a further down Broad Street, is unusual in Hay in being built of yellow brick. These so-called 'London bricks' would have been brought in by train and are no doubt the reason for its name. When first built it was a shop run by William Terrett, grocer and corn merchant, who appears to have had a mill on Heol y Dwr in the early 1870s.[15]

Opposite Terrett's, on the other side of Broad Street, was another grocer's at No. 12, this one of long-standing. It had been run by a succession of people since at least 1841, but in 1891 was probably the premises of Price and Davies. On the census of that year Tom Davies, grocer, is shown as living there with a 15-year-old apprentice. By 1911 this shop was being run by Frank Cadman, miller, corn and seeds merchant, who was also running the Hay Mill further down the street.

The grocery trade was one of the few in Hay to be greatly boosted by the coming of the railway. The number of grocers in the town increased steadily from four in 1859 to 15 in 1895 as a host of new products began to pour in from Birmingham and the Midlands by train. Many products that today are household names were then novelties. Cadbury's chocolate, Chiver's jams, Bovril, Golden Shred marmalade and Jacobs Cream Crackers were all seen for the first time around this period, together with many more.

THOMAS WALLIS AND THE POST OFFICE, 1896
Broad Street's third grocer, in 1891, was at No. 6. Many grocers of the time added something like 'master baker', or 'confectioner' to their entry on the census, but Thomas Wallis at No. 6 was unique in adding 'ironmonger'. Perhaps he specialised in that side of the grocery trade that deals with cleaning products rather than food. The use of lye, vinegar and salt for laundry and household cleaning was rapidly becoming a thing of the past as Lux laundry soap and products like Colgate toothpaste, Reckitts Blue for whitening laundry and Robin starch for aprons and men's collars came onto the market.

Cleanliness was much on the mind of people in the latter part of the nineteenth century. In 1880 there had been an outbreak of scarlet fever in the town, attributed to insanitary conditions, and further outbreaks of this and

measles occurred in 1895 and 1896. Schools were closed in these years for 16, and a massive 25 weeks respectively on the orders of the Medical Officer of Health.[16]

The issue of street cleaning and waste disposal was dealt with when, in 1895, a contract at five shillings a week was awarded to William Lilwall, a haulier who lived on Heol y Dwr, for collecting the dust and scrapings from the streets, and household ashes. It was arranged that the ash cart was to go through the streets twice a week and house refuse was to be carted to the river.[17] The streets thus became cleaner while the river suffered.

The initials of Thomas Wallis inset into the wall of the new post office he built in 1896

School closures meant that No. 6, where Thomas Wallis and his wife were living, became more crowded than ever. By 1891 the couple had seven children and were accommodating a lad who helped in the shop, together with two girl servants aged 13 and 18. They would go on to have 12 children altogether, ten girls and two boys.

Thomas Wallis may have been dissatisfied with the grocery and ironmongery trades, however, for when a house fire did extensive damage to the premises in 1893 he took it as an opportunity to launch himself on a whole new career. He had a small building erected beside No. 6, taking up half the entryway to do so, and in 1896 opened this as a post office and telephone exchange.[18] His initials and the date are recorded on the front wall. A safe was built into the back wall of No. 6 and its former stables were used to house the large batteries needed for the telephones. With access from the first floor of No. 6 the new building also provided an extra bedroom for his continually growing family.

Thomas Wallis's enthusiasm for his new career evidently communicated itself to his daughters, almost all of whom would go on to be post office workers, in one place or another. The Hay post office and telephone exchange would not remain on Broad Street, however. They were transferred to the Pavement when Thomas Wallis retired and moved his family to Poplar House.

OVERLEAF: A c.1900 view down Bridge Street from the south side of Broad Street, by Alfred Watkins. (Image courtesy of Hereford Libraries)

5

The Café Royal and the First World War

Q UEEN Victoria died on 22 January 1901 and Hay's long-serving vicar, Archdeacon Bevan, retired later that same year. Victoria had reigned for 64 years and Bevan had guided the spiritual and temporal lives of the people of Hay for most of them. Now, however, he was 81 and it was time to make way for a younger man. He and his family were living at Hay Castle and would continue to do so. The church authorities had to find somewhere else for the new vicar to live.

Broad Street in 1901. West House is on the far left with Prospect House beyond the tree. Part of the Three Tuns in the foreground on the right is followed by a narrow gap for Bridge Street, the Black Swan and then No. 6

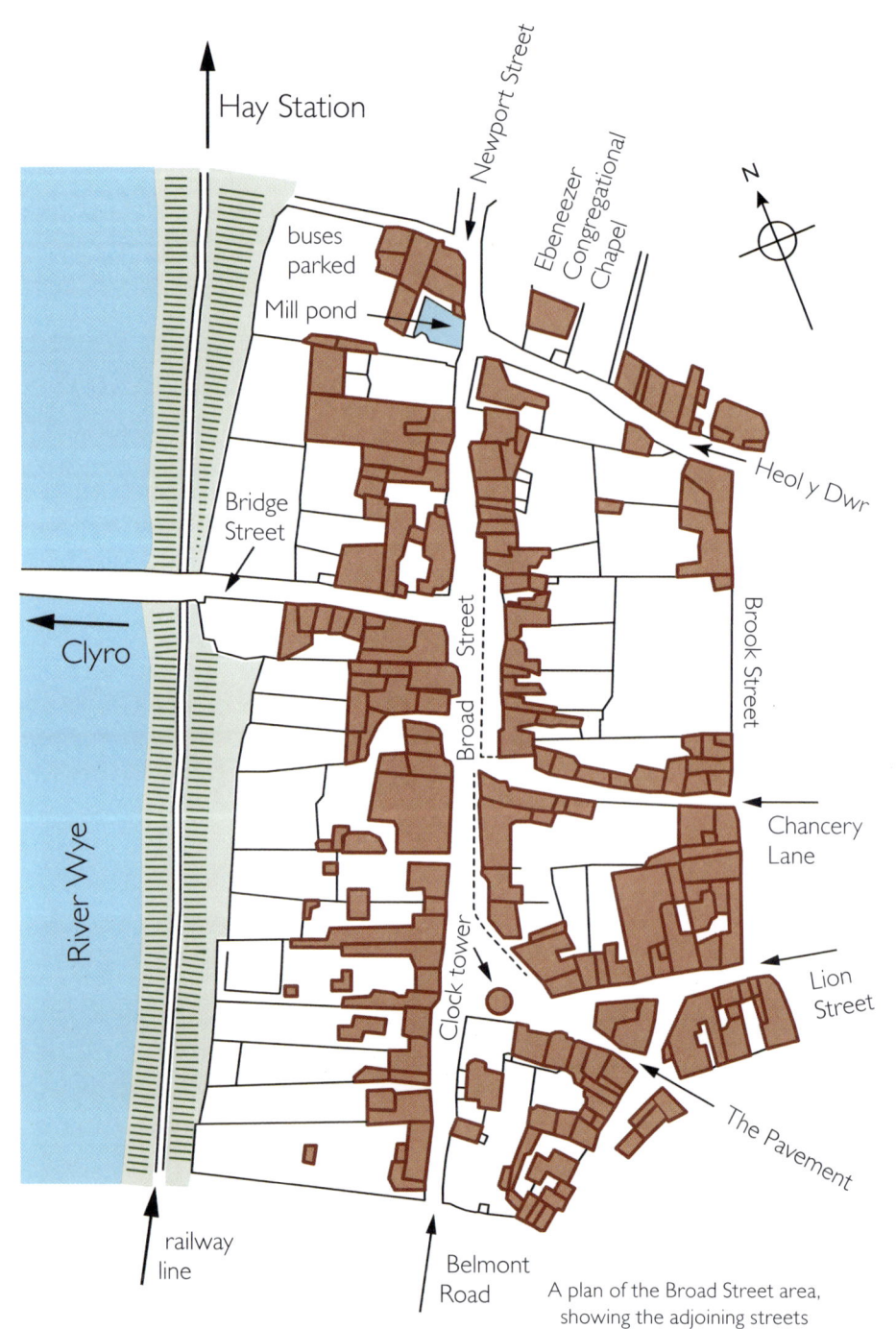

A plan of the Broad Street area, showing the adjoining streets

The year 1901 also saw the birth of a baby who would, like Archdeacon Bevan, hold a place in the affections of Hay people for many years, albeit for different reasons. Billie Pugh was born in the December of 1901, which was bitterly cold. Snow was piled high in the streets and a blizzard was blowing when his mother went into labour in West House on Broad Street. She was no longer young, her eldest child was already 20, and her daughter was worried. Would the midwife be able to get down from Castle Street? But Billie Pugh was born safely and would grow up to keep a much-loved shop on the Pavement for four decades, selling sweets, home-made ice-cream and tobacco. His son and grandson keep a television shop in the next-door premises today.

Across the road from West House, at No. 6, Thomas Wallis and his 22-year-old daughter were running the Post Office. Six other daughters and two young sons were still at home but although the family was so large, and still growing, they decided not to keep for their own use the room where the grocers-cum-ironmongery had been. Instead, they would try and get some income from it. There was a 'Shop to Let' sign in the window.

The Pugh family moved across to Bridge Street after a while, and Billie would walk from there to his school on the Brecon Road, a journey fraught with hazards. In later life he would tell of dodging the contents of chamber pots emptied into the street out of bedroom windows and tripping over men lying in the gutters, still dead drunk from the night before.[1] Wages were low but cider was cheap and there were more than 30 pubs in Hay serving a population of under 2,000.

Broad Street was dangerous for other reasons too. Billie was ten when a roof tile fell on him and he would bear a deep scar at the top of his forehead for the rest of his life.

❖❖

ACCIDENT

On Saturday morning last a little boy named Billie Pugh, son of Mr and Mrs Pugh, of No.1 Bridge Street, was playing with several of his companions outside the Café Royal Restaurant in Bridge St when a tile from the roof fell on his head, inflicting a nasty gash on the side of the skull and causing it to bleed profusely. The little fellow was for a short time unconscious, but he is now making satisfactory progress under the care of Dr Hincks.[2]

◆◆◆

The Café Royal was not on Bridge Street as the paper claimed. Bridge Street was where Billie Pugh lived. It was in fact at No. 6 Broad Street and the woman running it in 1911 was called Sarah Ann Hitchcox.

She had been born Sarah Ann Lane in 1874, in Bearwood, Herefordshire, one of a family of 13. Her father earned barely enough to feed them, though he was the head man on a farm, but they managed to save a shilling a week nonetheless. The virtue of thrift was deeply ingrained.

Sarah Ann had gone into service on leaving school, along with the thousands of other unmarried females who were compelled to live as servants in the households of their employers at that time. But her independent spirit was chafed by the restrictions imposed on her as a cook in Whitney Rectory, and after a while she left. A Brecon bakery took her on and this was better, but still did not offer the scope she craved. So, with the dawning of the Edwardian era she took a brave decision. She would open a café of her own.

Starting a business was not something that most women of her generation would have thought of attempting. The conventions of the time required them to aim almost solely at marriage. Even apart from that, however, the obstacles were formidable. Sarah Ann had little in the way of capital, the risk of ending up in debt was high, and debt carried a heavy social stigma. But she was determined.

One morning in 1902, therefore, she took a train from Brecon to Hay and found herself standing in front of No. 6 Broad Street with its 'Shop to Let' sign in the window. It looked hopeful. So, the following week she went back again, this time taking two of her sisters with her, and the three of them inspected the place from the inside. They tried to imagine it as a café. A gas cooker would be needed, and a table for food preparation. Some tables and chairs for customers would have to be acquired. But then, with the addition of a tin bath behind a screen for the washing up, it would be at least functional. Sarah Ann could be in business with only a small initial outlay. She decided to take it on and give it the same name as the Brecon bakery – the Café Royal.

And it worked. For the first year or so Sarah Ann managed to run her café successfully. She only had the one room but it was enough. When Thomas Wallis retired and moved his family to Poplar House, however, she had a difficult decision to make. Should she take over the whole of No. 6 – or not? It would be a big step. She consulted Robert Griffiths, the solicitor across the road, and his advice has been remembered by members of the Hitchcox family ever since. 'I wouldn't take on that old place if I were you.'

The building was certainly old. It had been built around 1623, and the house fire of 1893 hadn't done it much good. But, having asked for Robert Griffiths' advice, Sarah Ann found the courage to ignore it. She took on the whole building and, together with her sisters, opened a second dining room, this one overlooking the street from the first floor.

But it was a struggle. An agricultural depression in 1903 caused a drop in wages and it was only the fact that they were serving some of the big houses in the area that kept Hay businesses afloat. By 1904 Sarah Ann was ready to give it all up and emigrate to New Zealand. She was 30 and unmarried.

Meanwhile, as Sarah Ann was preparing to leave the street, a new couple were arriving to take up residence in Belle Vue. Charles Griffiths had sold it to the church authorities for £1,500, after living there for something like 45 years, and it was now to be the vicarage for St Mary's Church. The view down the length of Broad Street was about to be enjoyed by Hay's new vicar, the Revd J.J. de Winton and his new wife.

Perhaps the idea of marriage was catching that year, for Sarah Ann's dreams of New Zealand ended when an outstandingly good-looking young

Frank Edward Hitchcox.
(Photo courtesy of Neil Hitchcox)

insurance agent called Frank Edward Hitchcox arrived in Hay and went up to her top dining room. She was a good cook and his exclamation, when he paid the bill, was spontaneous. 'By golly, I enjoyed that meal! I wouldn't mind marrying the woman who cooked it!'

'My grandmother took his money,' says Sarah Ann's grandson, Neil, 'and replied "Well, I cooked it myself."' They were married three weeks later. 'How he got a job as an insurance agent we'll never know,' continues Neil,

> because he had served his apprenticeship as a gardener at Blenheim Palace. His father was a shepherd on a big estate near Finstock, Oxfordshire, and they were a poor family, living in the most basic of small cottages with a thatched roof and stone floor. Frank had left school as soon as he could read and write, aged nine.

Once married, Frank opened a grocery shop in the building that had been the post office, and they called it the XL Stores on their letter-heading: X for the last letter of his surname and L for the first letter of her maiden name,

The XL Stores with Eric Hitchcox standing in the doorway in a long white apron, and Sarah Ann in the doorway of the Café Royal with daughter, Nancy. The other two are relatives, Frank and Miriam. (Photo courtesy of Neil Hitchcox)

Lane. The shop was run jointly with the café under a legally constituted business partnership, and in the years to come Frank would give Sarah Ann cause to be thankful for this. Had she taken on the role of subordinate wife, as was more usual at that time, the family would have come to grief.

For the first years of the marriage all went well. It was still a good time to be in the grocery trade, as dozens of new and highly marketable products continued to pour in, thanks to the railways – though the Hitchcoxes' neighbour, Caleb Kedward, was deeply resentful about the unlooked-for competition from the XL Stores in spite of this. His own grocery shop was just the other side of the entry between them. There wasn't a lot he could do, but when Frank put in a side-window he sent him a bill for 1/6d a week for the daylight coming in from the entry. It was never paid, of course, but he had at least managed to express his conviction that Frank owed him something.

Mr Kedward stands outside his grocery shop at No. 8 (now the Small Farms butcher's with bay windows on the upper floors). The side window put in by Frank Hitchcox can be seen on the right

By 1911, the year the tile fell on Billie Pugh's head, Caleb Kedward had moved further up the street to No. 14. He must have continued in the grocery trade from there, for when Billie left school he took him on as an apprentice, though the arrangement did not last long. Billie disliked being an errand boy for the tyrannical, bad-tempered Mr Kedward and soon left, much to his father's chagrin. Mr Pugh senior was a Victorian father, strict and censorious.

He took Billie on himself, making him an apprentice boot and shoemaker, but that did not last either. It was in his elder brother John's fish shop on Lion

Street that Billie would find his metier. The marble slab they used for the fish is still there under a covering in the window of Hay Deli. Shopkeeping suited Billie Pugh. He would open his sweet shop on the Pavement in 1934.

Frank and Sarah Ann Hitchcox had been married for seven years by the time the 1911 census was taken. They had a son, Eric, who was six, and two daughters, Sylvia and Ruth Francis, aged four and seven months. A 15-year-old niece from Dilwyn lived in and helped in the shop, and a 14-year-old cousin of Eric's, also named Frank Hitchcox, acted as errand boy.

Messrs F.E. and S.A. Hitchcox, as the War Tribunal would later call them, had added a bakery to their joint business interests by that time. Commercial products might be taking over the grocery shelves, but the bread and cakes in the window of the Café Royal were all produced in their own bakehouse. The small brick building they had put up in the garden behind the Café Royal was producing such quantities of bread and cakes that Frank felt entitled to describe himself as a baker and confectioner on the census, though he never did any baking. For unspecified health reasons he was unable to even enter the bakehouse. Neil remembers him as a delicate, anxious man who fainted easily.

Frank would later tell the wartime tribunal that his doctor had suggested he take up farming to improve his health. The story is told by his granddaughter, Jennifer, of how he found himself at an auction one day and decided on a whim to buy a farm at Westbrook in the Golden Valley, just beyond Hardwicke. When he got home Sarah Ann asked him how he was going to pay for it and he replied easily 'You'll manage somehow'. It was a foretaste of things to come.

Sarah Ann and Frank had three children by 1911, but the Revd J.J. de Winton and his wife had five under the age of eight. A nurse, a nursemaid, a cook and a parlour maid all lived in to help look after them, and it was fortunate that the Revd de Winton had arranged for some cows to be put onto the glebe lands down near St Mary's to provide milk. The railway might be bringing in most kinds of goods but it was unable to cope with fresh milk. With the use of electricity still in its infancy, there was no refrigeration and the chances of bacteria multiplying in transit were high. It would not be until April 1913 that local contractor, William Lilwall, would get permission to lay electricity cables in Broad Street.[3]

Stephen Meredith Jones in the doorway of his shop at London House. He must have moved here later in 1911 for he gives this as his family's address in the census for that year. Later he would also take on the premises next door, previously the Old White Lion.
(Photo courtesy of Ken Jones)

In a further effort to keep his family safe, the Revd de Winton had asked, in 1907, that the speed of cars down Belmont Road be limited to four miles an hour.⁴ A new form of tarmac, patented around the turn of the century, was making the roads smooth at last and the speed of cars was rising dramatically. Belle Vue's front door opened almost straight onto this narrow road and with no pavement at this point it was a dangerous place for small children.

Further down the road, Broad Street's newest solicitor in 1907 had come up from Devon to work with Edmund Hall Cheese, who was aging. In fact they had gone into partnership after a six-month trial period and Herbert Rowse Armstrong had then married on the strength of his new position. He was of slight, almost boyish build, and lively; popular with local people. He took over Cheese's role drilling the Volunteer force in the Drill Hall and was made up to Captain. He also joined the Freemasons and was Grand Master for a term.

Only his home life was perhaps not all he might have wanted it to be. In their wedding photos he and his wife appear ill-matched. She looks rather as if she might have felt more at home in a gown and mortar board than in her lacy white wedding clothes, while he is so slight as to seem like a boy beside her.

On the 26 April 1914 Edmund Hall Cheese died of prostate cancer and, when his wife died the following day of a heart attack, Armstrong inherited the whole practice. In the years to come his name would bring Hay to the forefront of national attention for the first time in its 800-year history.

War with Germany was declared on 4 August, 1914 and on 13 August the local paper would report that 'Capt H. Rowse Armstrong, of Hay, who a few weeks ago went on a holiday tour in Switzerland, is unable to get across the border, and is therefore unable to return home.'⁵ Within a few weeks he would sign up to serve in the army although he need not have done so. Enlistment was voluntary and at 45 he was at the upper end of the acceptable age range. He had also gone on holiday by himself, leaving his wife at home with two small children, when he had only just acquired sole responsibility for his solicitor's practice. It seems as though he felt the need to get away.

THE FIRST WORLD WAR

Young Bernard Jones, son of Stephen Meredith Jones, the tailor, was only 15 when war was declared in August 1914, but he was keen to enlist. His elder brother, Spencer, soon signed up and he was eager to do the same. Boys were supposed to be 18 to enlist, however, and 19 to serve abroad so it looked as if he would have to wait.

Stephen Meredith Jones, the tailor, with his wife, Emily. Their six sons – Trevor, Ivor, Geoffrey, Spencer, Ralph and Bernard – were all born within nine years. Ivor and Ralph had health issues and were unable to sign up, and Geoffrey was too young. The other three all went to war and returned safely. (Photo courtesy of Ken Jones)

But exhortations from prominent local men, public meetings and martial parades made the waiting ever more difficult. War fever raged across the country and the Revd J.J. de Winton went so far as to denounce from the pulpit those middle-class youths who failed to sign up as 'criminal, callous and cowardly'.[6]

Bernard's father had moved his family and tailoring business down from the Pavement to London House in 1911, so when a lively public meeting was held round the clock tower it was right outside Bernard's home (*see overleaf*). As a patrol leader in the Boy Scouts he was present at the meeting anyway, along with Scoutmaster, Rhys Harding. The two stood listening

This photo from 1911 shows the ceremony during which the people of Hay in Huron, Canada, presented a flag to the people of Hay; however, the meeting held here to drum up support for the First World War would have looked much the same, with speakers on a raised podium in front of the clock tower. London House on the left-hand side of the photo is here still Charles Terrett's, the grocers

as rousing speeches were made and bands played stirring tunes. Councillor Thomas Stokoe, aged 36, of Prospect House, gave an impassioned speech and was met with hearty cheers when he announced that he had put his name down for service. Many were so moved that they signed up on the spot. Tom Stokoe had no intention of actually serving, but that would only become apparent later.

Another stirring event occurred when the Hay Territorials went off to coastal duties in Pembrokeshire:

Vast crowds from the countryside and town lined the Streets as the Territorials, over 70 strong, preceded by the Hay bands playing patriotic airs, marched to the station. The platforms and bridge were packed with friends and relatives, as there was scarcely a house from which someone had not gone, in some cases 3 and 4 from one house.[7]

It was all too much for Bernard, and by the morning of 19 June 1915 he could wait no longer. He got the train to Brecon as if going to school as usual but went instead to the army recruiting office where he told them he was 18 and wanted to join up. He was tall enough to be 18 and they put his name down unquestioningly. He was enrolled as Private Bernard Darwin Jones 22511 in the 11th Battalion of the South Wales Borderers, and six months later was in France, landing at Le Havre on 4 December 1915, shortly after his 17th birthday.

His son, Ken, tells the story of how some years later an official came to inspect Bernard's birth certificate and assumed that he had been one of the thousands joining up to escape grinding poverty at home. 'You can't really blame him for running away, can you?' he said. 'Anyone would run away from a start in life like that, born on the pavement.' It was an understandable mistake. His mother had given the family address as simply 'the Pavement' when she registered his birth in November 1898.

Bernard Jones served in the South Wales Borderers. His older brother, Trevor, was in the Welsh Guards. (Photo courtesy of Ken Jones)

Three months after landing in France, Bernard was the subject of a *Brecon County Times* headline:

HAY BOY'S SPLENDID COURAGE
REMARKABLE COINCIDENCE

He had walked into a First Aid post on 2 March 1916, saying 'the beggars have shot me', and he had in fact been shot in the back, the bullet emerging from his lower chest. Yet he somehow managed to walk on to the advanced dressing station, laughing and joking with men of the field ambulance. The remarkable coincidence of the headline was that their sergeant in the R.A.M.C. was Bernard's former Scoutmaster, Rhys Harding. 'I wish I had been there to see him,' he would write home. 'The medical officer at the advanced dressing station said he was the pluckiest lad that had ever passed through his hands.'[8] Bernard was invalided home and sent to Norwich Hospital, his wound so serious that he was still recovering three months later.

Back in Hay, the lanterns had been removed from most of the street lights and the fever of volunteering had given way to conscription. The Revd J.J. de Winton was 18 months older and somewhat more temperate in his views. Being in Holy Orders he was exempt from being called up himself, but was required to sit on the Local Tribunal and give judgement on applications for exemption. It was morally and emotionally demanding. Decisions had to be made on the fate of friends, neighbours and parishioners; decisions that could mean life or death, or cause businesses to close down for lack of manpower, and take away livelihoods.

The case of Councillor Thomas Stokoe was one that set the tribunal against the army again and again. He had made a great display of having signed up with the army at the start of the war, but had then persuaded the tribunal to grant him a stay of execution. His gift for oratory, honed whilst training as a barrister, had stood him in good stead. He owned the Crown Hotel, he said, and the Lamb Inn. He ran a grocers, a soft drinks manufactory and bottling plant, and he was a dispensing chemist under the National Insurance Act. He also occupied 50 acres of land in Radnorshire from which he ran a milk run in Hay. The tribunal were won over, and when service became compulsory in January 1916 they granted him complete exemption.

But the military appealed immediately on the grounds that he should find someone else to run his businesses for him as other men did. Complete exemption was therefore amended and he was given six months to arrange this, but again the military appealed. Their representative, Capt.

Mavrojani, protested vehemently that six months was too long. None of Stokoe's businesses gave him certified occupation status and it was not right for a bachelor to remain at home whilst married men had to go as soldiers. 'Why', he demanded of Stokoe, 'did you attest [sign up] in the first place? Was it your intention when you signed this form to appeal? You never intended to go as a soldier, you intended to go to the Tribunal?' And Stokoe readily agreed that this was so. He had intended to appeal all along, believing that he couldn't get an exemption unless he had first attested. The Chairman of the Tribunal backed him up saying that many people had believed this and the Government had never contradicted it. Capt. Mavrojani's jaw dropped.

> And you took 2/9 for one day's Army pay?
>   Yes [*laughter*]
> And that is all you want to do for the army?

The Tribunal retired to consider the matter, and on their return the Chairman dismissed Capt. Mavrojani's appeal. Mr Stokoe was clearly a many-sided man, he said, with a level of eloquence that made it a pity he had not remained as a barrister. This was followed by more laughter and his exemption was allowed to stand. Capt. Mavrojani was left grinding his teeth.[9]

Bernard was well enough to visit his family on Broad Street in June 1916, but was back in France and on the Somme at the beginning of July. His battalion had been incorporated into the 38th (Welsh) Division, raised by Lloyd George, and was heading for its first major engagement.

The battle for Mametz Wood would be one of the bloodiest of the entire war. The 38th were a volunteer section composed largely of clerks, colliers and farmers, and they were untrained for this kind of warfare. The German troops were well-trained, well-equipped professional soldiers and included a large contingent of the famous Prussian Guard. They were hidden in the wood whilst the 38th had to cross an open valley to get to them. The prospect was terrifying.

The battle lasted five gruelling, blood-soaked days. Some 4,000 men of the 38th were machine-gunned down in just three days. A thousand men died through a failure in communication that sent them walking, not running, across the valley in broad daylight without even a smoke screen to cover them. But the wood was, finally, taken. The Welsh Memorial that stands today overlooking that open valley is a red dragon on a plinth holding barbed wire in its claws.

Miraculously, Bernard Jones came through the Somme offensive without injury. Sgt Rhys Harding R.A.M.C., however, was not so lucky. He was wounded in France and invalided home to hospital in September 1916. Sent back to France on recovering, he had 'the thrilling experience,' said the *Brecon County Times* euphemistically, 'of being on a twice torpedoed vessel'.

Bernard's father had three sons and three employees serving in the war by April 1916, and his tailoring business was suffering. Lloyd George was recommending that women be allowed into jobs previously held only by men, and the huge new munitions factory at Rotherwas in Hereford was employing them very successfully: 4,000 women would be working there by the end of the war, including many from Hay. They could get a train to Barrs Court Station in Hereford and from there a dedicated train would take them on to Rotherwas free of charge. Women would eventually provide 80% of Britain's munitions in the First World War.

Stephen Jones therefore decided to try the experiment of employing a woman himself. He took on Elsie Lewis of No. 2 St Mary's Villas as an apprentice tailor and found that she quickly became skilled. While the men sat cross-legged on cushions on the floor in the traditional way, Elsie was set to work in a separate room where she would eventually specialise in waistcoats, though she could do more or less anything required. His father's employment of her was to have a profound effect on Bernard when he came home after the war.

In the meantime, older and yet older men were being called on to serve as the war progressed. In August 1918 even Bernard's father received his papers, although he was by this time in his 50th year. The Tribunal granted him a conditional exemption, but it was altogether a nerve-racking time.

When the war finally ended in November 1918 a grand ball was held in the Agricultural Hall (now the Richard Booth Bookshop) in Lion Street. Sarah Ann Hitchcox and her sisters, Fanny, Taddy and Elizabeth, catered for the 500 people attending and they provided hot food, cooked at the Café

Royal and carried round in tea chests packed with straw to keep the heat in.

And the men began to return. All three of the Jones sons who had served came back, Bernard still only 19 years and 11 months when he was demobbed. The 38th (Welsh) had been held back from active service overseas for almost a year after their ordeal at Mametz Wood, but had been back in France for the Battle of Ypres, and again Bernard had come through unscathed.

He came home to find Elsie Lewis, her brother and the three of his own brothers who had not gone to war all employed by his father. There was no room for him, even had that been what he wanted. Ivor, the eldest brother, had always been crippled and would die in September 1919, which might have left room for Bernard, but by this time he had begun work as an insurance agent in Brecon and chose to remain there. He bought a motorbike and, having come through all the carnage of the war, lost a leg in an accident. He had a very good prosthetic fitted, however, and the loss handicapped him only a little.

Bernard had decided that Elsie Lewis was the one for him on the instant he first met her, and so it turned out. She rejected the hopeful advances of other young men and married Bernard nine years later at the Salem Baptist Chapel on Bell Bank, Hay. It had taken all that time for him to get sufficiently established in civilian life. Their first child, Kenneth Bernard Meredith Jones was born on 3 February 1929 at the house of her parents opposite the church, and he was followed by Daphne, Rex and Ivor.

Bernard's time with the forces was far from over, however. In 1938, while his brothers Ralph and Geoffrey ran the tailoring business on Broad Street, he took a full-time job as an Executive Officer with the Hereford, Brecknock and Radnor Territorial Army. At that time it was based in the Drill Hall, almost opposite No. 1 Garibaldi Terrace where he was living with his family. When the Second World War broke out he became involved in the Local Defence Volunteers, later renamed the Home Guard, and was promoted to Major. For services to the three counties he would later be awarded an MBE. He finally retired in 1964, leaving his son Ken to carry on his work as Executive Officer to the Territorial Army for the next 40 years, combining it with volunteer work as a Justice of the Peace.

Councillor Thomas Stokoe died in 1919. He had managed to evade the clutches of the army for the whole of the war, but was caught instead by the gambling bug and lost a great deal of money. Most of his gambling had taken place at the Lamb Inn at the bottom of Newport Street, which he himself owned.

6

The Armstrong Case

CAPT. H. Rowse Armstrong had been promoted during the course of the war and would return home, eventually, as Major Armstrong, retaining the title even in civilian life. In the meantime, however, he opted for a further posting when the war ended, apparently in no hurry to get back to either his family or his solicitor's practice on Broad Street.

When he did finally return, in May 1921, it was at the request of his wife, Katharine, who was having, she said, a return of her nervous troubles. He went willingly, for there was undoubtedly affection between them, although he was irritated by her tendency towards what he saw as neuroticism. Nine months later, however, she would be dead, and ten months after that he would find himself at the centre of a court case that would electrify the nation.

Armstrong was arrested, on New Year's Eve 1921, on a charge of attempting to poison Oswald Martin, a solicitor who worked with Robert Griffiths at the

Major Herbert Rowse Armstrong. (Photo courtesy of William Beales & Co.)

practice opposite to his own across Broad Street (now Gabb & Co). The case was far from clear-cut, however. It was true that Oswald Martin had become ill after taking tea with Major Armstrong, but Dr Hincks had declared him to be suffering from nothing worse than a bilious attack and the whole affair would then have been forgotten if Oswald Martin's father-in-law had not become involved.

He was Fred Davies, the chemist whose shop was at the top of the Pavement (where there is still a chemist's today). But Davies lived at No. 1 Belmont Road, two doors up from Tinto House on Broad Street where Dr Hincks lived, and he called round to see him. 'My wife and I believe', he told Dr Hincks, 'that Armstrong handed Oswald a scone laced with arsenic when they were having tea together. Armstrong intends to do him in. We are sure of it. The worry is making us ill.'[1]

It sounded ludicrous – and in any case Oswald Martin's symptoms had not been consistent with arsenic poisoning. Dr Hincks brushed the idea aside. But Fred Davies was not to be put off. 'How about', he suggested, 'we get Oswald to give a urine sample and send it to be analysed? That way we can be sure one way or the other. And by the way', he added, 'Oswald and our daughter were sent a box of chocolates anonymously and one of their dinner guests was ill after eating them. Perhaps we should get them tested as well. It might have been Armstrong that sent them.'

Dr Tom Hincks was reluctant, but Fred Davies was a neighbour and what harm could it do? He gave in. Davies took a bottle from his chemist's shop and Oswald Martin provided a urine sample. Then he, Hincks, sent this to the Home Office in London together with the box of chocolates, confident within himself that it was all a waste of time. When the results came back showing traces of arsenic in both the urine sample and the chocolates, then, he was shaken.

Did it occur to him that Fred Davies might have doctored them? Arsenic was a widespread commodity at that time. Davies had plenty of it in his shop and had certainly had the opportunity to tamper with both the bottle in which the urine sample was taken, and with the chocolates. He was also antagonistic towards Armstrong. The reasons were not entirely clear, though they might have been connected with Armstrong helping another chemist to set up in competition.

Fred Davies had had his chemist's shop on the corner of High Town and Cranbourne Alley (the Pavement) since the 1890s. It is still a chemist's shop today

But if these thoughts crossed Dr Hincks's mind, he did not voice them. Asked by the Home Office to meet with the Director of Public Prosecutions, he took a train to Hereford and signed a written statement which included a judgement on Armstrong that would subsequently help to send him to the gallows.

> I think the man is a homicidal maniac and if he gets to know these questions are the subject of police or other investigations he may destroy himself, his children, Mr Martin and me.²

It was an extraordinary statement for a family doctor to make to the police, in front of the DPP, about a patient who had shown no inclination towards violence, as far as we know. Certainly, the prosecution did not invite him to expand upon it at either of Armstrong's trials.

But Hincks was desperate to ensure that all enquiries into the alleged poisoning incident were kept secret. If it got about that he and Fred Davies had initiated legal action against Armstrong, and Armstrong turned out to be innocent, then his reputation as a trusted family doctor would be in tatters. The Home Office understood that he ran the risk of being ruined by the enquiries that were now bound to take place and duly enforced complete secrecy until the day of the arrest.

Meanwhile, a story gained currency at that time that two Scotland Yard detectives had watched Armstrong's comings and goings across Broad Street from the top of the clock tower. If they were there on the morning of New Year's Eve, 1921, they would have seen him emerge from Chancery Lane, cross Broad Street and go into his office. Although it was a Saturday, he was planning to work for a couple of hours before returning home to his children. With no idea that he was under any kind of suspicion, it never crossed his mind that he would never see them or his home again. But the police had investigated as much as they could without alerting him and now they were about to close in.

Armstrong was used to dealing with the police in his capacity as Clerk to the Magistrates. So when the Deputy Chief Constable of Hereford walked into his office that Saturday morning with the two Scotland Yard detectives he was friendly and ready to be helpful. Only gradually did the full horror of his position begin to dawn on him. It took six hours, during which he was kept without food or refreshment, but finally he was arrested on the charge that two months previously he had attempted to poison Oswald Martin with arsenic. He walked with the police round to the police station on Heol y Dwr and was locked up, never to know freedom again.

The former courthouse and police station on Heol y Dwr, now a private dwelling

Detail of the barred cell window in the north elevation

Sitting alone in his cell through the miserable Sunday that followed, he must have realised that his standing in the community was irreparably damaged, no matter what happened from then on. He was a war veteran, church warden, former grand master of the Hay Lodge, Clerk to the Magistrates of Hay, Painscastle and Bredwardine, popular with local people and a pillar of society – but mud sticks. Even the hot meal taken to him by Frank Hitchcox from the Café Royal can have done little to raise his spirits.

'The news of his arrest hit the town like a bombshell,' a successor in his legal practice, Martin Beales, would write 50 years later. 'There was no other topic of conversation in any house or pub for miles around.'[3] Was it likely that this well-liked and respected professional man would have tried to poison someone? It beggared belief. A large crowd assembled in Heol y Dwr on Monday morning to give him three rousing cheers as he stepped from the courtroom into the taxi waiting to take him to Worcester Gaol. Somewhere along the line a mistake must have been made. They were convinced of it.

But Dr Tom Hincks was no better off once Armstrong had been arrested, for his practice would still be in jeopardy if Armstrong were found not guilty at trial. He had walked into a trap of his own making, and now he had a strong incentive for doing everything in his power to ensure that Armstrong was convicted.

Armstrong was forced to endure two trials. The first was heard before Hay Magistrates Court on Heol y Dwr for a decision on whether or not there was a case to answer, and it must have been a torment to him. Proceedings were drawn out to an inordinate degree by the Crown prosecutor, and each successive day brought a fresh revelation that redounded to his discredit. The national newspapers had a field day.

But almost all the so-called revelations would turn out to be untrue. It was, for example, claimed that Armstrong had syphilis when Dr Hincks gave evidence that he had been treating him for this disease. But the diagnosis was wrong. It would turn out that Hincks had been giving Armstrong a course of painful injections for a disease he had never had. The jury at Armstrong's second and final trial, at Hereford Assize Court, were never told this, however. They were left with the impression that Armstrong had had syphilis and must therefore have been unfaithful to his wife. It was just one of several ways in which Armstrong's reputation as an honourable man had been ruined before his case ever came before the Assize Court at Hereford.

Hincks' contention that Armstrong was a homicidal maniac had by this time been taken far more seriously than he could have foreseen. He had given 'natural causes' as the reason for Armstrong's wife, Katharine, dying the year before and nobody had questioned that. Now, however, when Fred and Laura Davies put forward the idea that Armstrong might have killed her, they were listened to. Katharine Armstrong's body was exhumed and the eminent Home Office pathologist, Sir Bernard Spilsbury, was on hand to conduct a post-mortem examination. When he found that, after ten months in the ground, her body still contained a fatal dose of arsenic, the charge against Armstrong was amended. He was no longer charged with attempting to poison Oswald Martin – that case had always been a weak one in any case. He now stood before the Hereford Assize Court accused of murdering his wife.

Sir Bernard Spilsbury stayed overnight with Dr Tom Hincks in Tinto House on Broad Street, and the strength of the bond they formed is reflected in the extent to which Hincks' evidence in court would mirror that of the famous pathologist. He backed Spilsbury in asserting that the fatal dose of arsenic was almost certainly administered within 24 hours of Katharine's death, although he had no experience of his own to draw on in making this claim. It was an opinion that would be convincingly disputed in court, and one that has been disputed even more convincingly since, but it was the one on which the verdict would hang.

Sir Bernard Spilsbury was pre-eminent in his field and forcefully assertive in his manner. Judge Darling could not bring himself to admit that the famous man might be over-confident, and his summing up therefore followed a simple line of logic. The fatal dose had been administered within 24 hours of Katharine's death. She was too ill by then to have taken it herself. Therefore Armstrong must be guilty of having given it to her. There was no-one else it could reasonably have been.

All his friends – and he had many – wrote in support of Major Armstrong, while Dr Hincks was left to feel the full force of his predicament. If the jury disagreed with the judge and found Armstrong innocent, then he, Hincks,

Armstrong arriving at court in Hereford, accompanied by policemen.
(Photo courtesy of William Beales & Co.)

would have to leave town. It was as simple as that. He had deeds for the sale of his practice drawn up and ready to be signed.

But, after a trial lasting ten days the jury took just 48 minutes to find Armstrong guilty. Such evidence as there was had all been circumstantial, but the judge's summing up had convinced them. He had more or less directed them to find Armstrong guilty, and they had done so.

Major Herbert Rowse Armstrong was hanged at Gloucester Gaol on 22 May, 1922, the only solicitor to be hanged in British history. He died protesting his innocence to the last. The Revd J.J. de Winton told reporters that on the eve of his execution Armstrong had said, 'I feel better now than ever I did. I realise that the end has come and I am prepared for it. I have no confession to make. I am an innocent man'.[4]

Dr Hincks never did sell his practice. He died ten years later after falling from his horse within sight of Armstrong's house, on the hill above Cusop Dingle. It was Fred Davies and his wife who left town soon after the trial. Katharine Armstrong's body was re-interred in Cusop churchyard, the grave left unmarked for fear of undue interest by sightseers.

At Madame Tussauds a waxwork of Armstrong was stood next to that of Dr Crippen in the Chamber of Horrors and there, to her shock and great dismay, his youngest daughter came upon it whilst she was still a child. No-one had told the Armstrong children what really happened to their father.

Thousands of words have since been written on what a local paper of the time described as 'the most sensational events ever known on the borders of Brecon and Radnor'. Dozens of newspaper and magazine articles have been published and several books. A film has been made and two television programmes went out in 2019.

The earliest books assumed Armstrong's guilt as a matter of course. One continually referred to him as 'the little man' and leaned heavily on hearsay about him being henpecked by Katharine. But in 1994 an award-winning book was published by Martin Beales, the solicitor who, curiously enough, both sat at Armstrong's desk on Broad Street and lived in his house in Cusop Dingle. He contended that the trial was unsound on several counts, not least the final summing-up by Judge Darling. He wrote:

> It would be hard to find a judge's summing-up in the annals of crime that was more perverse and damaging to any prisoner. Darling was a hanging judge and in the trial of Armstrong he excelled himself.[5]

The BBC programme *Murder Mystery and My Family,* broadcast on 28 November 2019, also found that the way in which Judge Darling had directed the jury made Armstrong's conviction for murder unsound. It concluded that he should not have been convicted as a result of that trial.

But it was Hay historian David Bennett who went the whole way and made a case for Armstrong's innocence. His book, *Major Injustice,* casts a fresh light on Katharine Armstrong's mental state. Judge Darling had dismissed out of hand the idea that she might have been suicidal. Bennett provides evidence that the idea of killing herself was never far from her mind in the latter stages of her life.

It is thought now that Katharine may have been suffering from Addison's disease, a condition in which the immune system turns on itself and starts to destroy the adrenal glands. Without the hormones produced by the adrenals the body cannot metabolise carbohydrates, fats or proteins and this leads to a weakening of the heart, muscle and nerve tissues. It usually proves fatal if not treated. All Katharine's multifarious symptoms can be seen as manifestations of this disease – including, most tellingly, the progressive darkening of the skin from which she suffered in the last year of her life.

The symptoms of Addison's tend to come and go, depending to some extent on the patient's levels of anxiety, and this can lend credibility to the idea that the symptoms have a mental or emotional origin. Confusion over whether her symptoms had some physical cause or were, in the parlance of the day, 'functional' (that is to say 'psychosomatic') caused Katharine Armstrong considerable distress and she was very reluctant to consult Dr Hincks, agreeing finally only at Armstrong's insistence.

When Hincks came and diagnosed the majority of her symptoms as functional (or, in his word at the trial, 'imaginary') in origin, therefore, it was exactly what she had feared. Hincks had her committed to an institution for the insane and it marked the beginning of the end for her. She did eventually manage to get home by pleading with Armstrong to come and rescue her ('My own dearest hubby, for pity's sake fetch me home'), but went downhill fast from then on, terrified of losing Armstrong's affection and being a burden to him and their children.

We will never know for certain what happened between Herbert and Katharine Armstrong. If the fatal dose of arsenic was ingested more than 24 hours before Katharine's death then she could have taken it herself. There was a packet of arsenic in the cupboard of the room where she had been giving lessons to her son the day before she took to her bed for the final time. Armstrong had been intending to use it for killing dandelions and would later find it had been unaccountably opened. Katharine also had a supply of arsenic in her bedroom cupboard that she had drawn from in order to mix her own homeopathic remedies. The police never investigated the contents of this cupboard.[6]

Armstrong had oscillated between an affectionate desire to be helpful to his wife and an irritable impatience with her seeming inability to 'buck up', as he put it. It is even possible that he assisted her death at her own request.

The hangman reported that his last words were 'I'm coming Katie'.

7

A Petrol Pump on the Pavement and the Second World War

THE 1920S

WHEN news of Armstrong's arrest broke on the front pages of the local and national newspapers, Hay was described as a quaint, old-fashioned little town. By the time of his death its name had become a by-word for murder and intrigue. Yet to the people who lived there it was neither. It was just the place where they earned a living, brought up their children and grew old, as it always had been. Something new that did occur in the 1920s, however, was a widespread enthusiasm for dancing and entertainments of all kinds after the horrors of the war.

Rhys Harding had survived the 'thrilling' experience of being on a twice-torpedoed vessel, to come back and continue as Scoutmaster, church organist and choirmaster, with Bernard Jones in the choir. Now, however, he also organised a drama group, put on a number of Gilbert and Sullivan operas, and formed a dance band. With himself on the piano and Tom Stokoe's brother, Freddy, on the drums, this band would become immensely popular throughout the region, and remain so all through the 1930s.

Freddy Stokoe is remembered today as a kindly, rather nervous, white-haired old gentleman. His brother, Councillor Tom Stokoe, had lost most of the family's money gambling, so Freddy scraped a living by working as a reporter for both the *Brecon County Times* and the *Hereford Times*, going to all the local funerals and spending a lot of time in the library. He is said to have been 'very big on Kilvert'.

There were a number of dance venues in Hay, but the main one in the early 1920s was the Drill Hall on Lion Street.

> Those were the days when dancers queued for the doors to open, and at 2 a.m. when the dance would be at its very zenith, there would frequently be a cap passed round for the band to play on until three o'clock.[1]

There were foxtrots and quicksteps, the waltz was back in fashion and the Charleston was fresh from America. Armstrong too had gone to dances in the Drill Hall after his wife died and he was a good dancer. With his boyish figure and twinkling blue eyes, he had had little trouble finding partners.

The Crown had a small ballroom, but it was on the first floor and used mainly by the wealthy families who took over the hotel for the fishing season. They would come to Hay by train bringing their furniture with them, and have it brought up from the station on carts.

The family who moved into the Three Tuns in 1922 might well have come because of those wealthy families at the Crown. Leslie Powell was a ghillie, a skilled fisherman who organised fishing trips for the gentry, and this gave him the means to support his family while he and his wife, Marion, were learning the pub trade.

Their daughter, Lucy, would go on to become one of Hay's most well-known 'characters', a living legend. She was three when her family arrived, but she would continue to live in the Three Tuns for the next 83 years. People would come from all over to visit both her and the pub itself, which she kept as an unspoilt reminder of a bygone era. Together they provided an atmosphere that was much valued. She never married. Her name would remain Lucy Powell to the day she died.

Her younger brother, Albert, was in his 97th year when he thought back over her life:

> She was a wonderful dancer when she was young – and a very strong swimmer. Lots of people swam at the Warren then. They had a diving board there. But she was a wonderful dancer. Waltzes, the foxtrot and that. They had dances at the Parish Hall in the '30s. Freddy Stokoe played the drums. She never married. Dad was a bit too hard on her. She was very attractive when she was young and lots of customers wanted to take her out but Dad wouldn't let her go till the pub closed and that was too late for them. Lucy and Dad were very close like. But she didn't have a lot of enjoyment.

The Powells managed to make a success of the Three Tuns in the early 1920s, though it was not easy. The town had upwards of 30 pubs, ten of them between the station and the clock tower alone. The Nelson (now Kingfisher House) was closest to Hay Station and the last one in England before the Welsh border. The first one in Wales was then the Bridge End Inn, on the bank of the Dulais. On Ship Pitch (Newport Street) were the Lamb and the Ship. And on Broad Street were the Tanners Arms, the Three Tuns, the Rose and Crown, the Seven Stars, the Old White Lion and, at the lower end of the Pavement, the Kings Head.

The Three Tuns could provide facilities for horses, but then so could half the others. The mounting block that is still outside the Bridge Street entrance was also remembered by Albert:

> People used to use the mounting block. There weren't so many cars in those days. People used to come in on horseback. We had stables at the back. We used to take the horses in and look after them. We charged sixpence a day for this. Some didn't like paying it. Some of these farmers were pretty tight mind.

But Leslie and Marion Powell did well in spite of the intense competition, and on 13 March 1925 they bought the Three Tuns from the Arnold Perrett brewery.[2]

The fire brigade and the town's undertakers were also still using horses in 1922, although this would soon change. The fire brigade consisted of volunteers who used a steam pump apparatus called Firefly (*see overleaf*) that was mounted on wheels pulled by two black horses belonging to George Barber of the Crown. They were pastured in a field on the other side of the bridge and would make off whenever anyone in uniform approached, frightened of having to attend another fire. A farm tractor replaced horses in 1925, but with its massive iron wheels and no tyres it did not represent much of an improvement in the efficiency of the service.

The same two black horses were used by Humphrey Vines Webb, known as HV, and his brother, Frank, to pull the hearse for their undertaking business. They were sons of the carriage builder James Webb who must have settled in Hay sometime before 1861 because he is listed on the census

The horse-drawn 'fire engine' called Firefly, heading past the Black Swan on Broad Street, pulled by two black horses belonging to George Barber of the Crown

for that year as a carpenter living at No. 21 Bear Street. James Webb would go on to establish a sizeable carriage-building business on Church Street, the site later occupied by Like's Garage and now the de Breos housing estate. HV and Frank had modernised the carriage business into a garage for motor vehicles and moved it to Lion Street.

The hearse for the undertaking side of their business, however, was kept on Broad Street. Back in 1920, HV had taken over a large shed built over a sloping earth floor where the long triangular pond had been filled in, and this housed the hearse together with one or two other vehicles. Today it is a carpentry workshop, but the board above the doors still lifts up to provide extra headroom for taller vehicles.

HV and Frank had been the undertakers who buried Katharine Armstrong in 1921, and the ones who had exhumed her body ten months later. HV had been the one to unscrew the lid of the coffin and find her face

The garage where H.V. Webb kept the hearse for his undertaking business, later this carpentry workshop

covered with a small silk handkerchief. He was present at the post mortem conducted by Sir Bernard Spilsbury, and a witness at the inquest where he confirmed that it was indeed Katharine's body. He also gave evidence at Armstrong's trial.

HV Webb bought No. 3 Broad Street in 1924 and installed two of his sisters there, with a petrol pump on the pavement outside (*see overleaf*). He and his wife, Mary Ann, had 13 children and the following year the youngest of them, named Humphrey after his father, went to work at his father and uncle's garage on Lion Street, aged just 13. He would continue there until he died and the garage was sold to Phil Gittins in 1979.

The Crown Hotel was struggling in the early 1920s. George Barber advertised the best accommodation, billiards, bowling, fishing, food, golfing, hunting, motoring and scenery (carefully listed in alphabetical order), with 20 guest bedrooms and parking for 20 cars. The days of livery stables at the rear were over. But it did little good; he could not make the place pay and in 1926 was declared bankrupt.

HV's sisters, Ethel aged 24 and Thelma aged 17, posing next to an early form of petrol pump on the pavement outside No. 3 Broad Street in 1924

The Hitchcoxes were also heading for trouble, though Sarah Ann was as yet unaware of it. She was spending most of her time in the hotel at the top of Belmont Road, which Frank had impulsively bought at auction, much as he had done with the farm at Westbrook. The Wye Hotel consisted of two premises combined into one. The old Cock Inn, once the office for the coal wharf (and now Jones Home Hardware), had been combined with the adjacent premises (now Red Indigo), to form a Temperance hotel, patronised mainly by travelling salesmen. The Temperance movement was thriving, for at that time the high levels of extreme poverty and domestic abuse prevalent in society were being attributed almost solely to drunkenness.

Behind the long street frontage of the Wye Hotel was a large room known as the Market Room where Sarah Ann continued to serve market day lunches. She could also derive additional income by hiring it out for Masonic meetings, children's parties and, most importantly, as a dance hall.

But it was hard work. Sarah Ann had had a fourth child, Nancy, in

The Red Indigo Indian Restaurant with part of Jones Home Hardware beyond on Castle Street were once combined in the Wye Temperance Hotel

her mid-40s and running the hotel whilst bringing up four children took some doing. Her granddaughter-in-law, Anne, tells how she happened by chance to meet a 93-year-old woman in a wheelchair in Newport, who had known Sarah Ann at this time. She had been employed at the Wye Hotel as a young teenager, she said, and she and a friend had been worked so hard that they had wanted to leave. So they had crept out of bed at two o'clock in the morning and walked all the way to Glasbury railway station, afraid that if they went to Hay Station they would be seen and sent back. But Sarah Ann worked her staff no harder than she worked herself and the Wye Hotel did pay its way. The trouble that was brewing for the family was on Broad Street, where Frank was in charge.

The crunch came one day in 1927 when Sarah Ann was called down to the Café Royal where their solicitor and bank manager were waiting to see her. She had been concentrating so much on the Wye Hotel that she had taken her eye off the ball of the family's finances as a whole and Frank had run up a debt of around £3,000. It was a huge amount, enough to have bought a house like Belle Vue twice over. Frank, said Sarah Ann, had 'got

Sarah Ann Hitchcox with her four children. The boy on the left is one of their cousins.
(Photo courtesy of Jennifer Powell)

above himself'. He had been shooting and fishing with 'the toffs', enhancing his film star looks with expensive clothes and providing hampers with bottles of Scotch for their picnics.

From Frank's point of view this had been an investment. He had been hoping to gather support for the sports field he had created on the northern side of the Brecon Road, with five tennis courts, a cricket pitch, a bowling green and a croquet lawn. He had also formed the Wye Hotel Sports Club, which offered shooting in season.

But in expecting extensive patronisation of the sports field on account of his fraternisation with the gentry, Frank was badly disappointed. His sports field was in competition with the tennis courts and bowling green in the centre of town and never became popular enough to justify the initial outlay. Maintenance costs were also high and, far from being an asset, the enterprise had turned out to be a serious drain on the family's resources.

F.E. & S.A. HITCHCOX
Proprietors of
Café Royal, 6 Broad Street, Hay
One Minute Walk from Railway Station

Wye Hotel, Castle Street, Hay
RESIDENTIAL, TOURIST AND COMMERCIAL HOTEL
(unlicensed)
Moderate Charges   Replete with every Home Comfort

FAMILY GROCERS,
BAKERS AND CONFECTIONERS

Estimates given for Catering, Public and Private Parties,
Irrespective of number

WYE HOTEL SPORTS CLUB

Cricket and Lawn Tennis Grounds

TERMS FOR SEASON:– Tennis (five courts) 12/6
Cricket 10/6, Croquet 5/- Bowls 5/-
Visitors 1/- per day or 2/6 per week

The Hotel can Provide Shooting in Season

Sarah Ann had known about the sports field but was taken aback by the size of the debt. She had two great assets, however. She had the gift of resilience, both physical and emotional, and her position in society allowed her to work. She was not, as Katharine Armstrong had been, condemned to languish in relative idleness as the wife of a middle-class professional man. She summoned all her resources and set to.

Women had played an important role outside the home during the war and now they were no longer hobbled by long skirts. In 1918 female householders over the age of 30 had even got the vote.[3] It all helped Sarah Ann to find the courage to do what she felt was needed. She dissolved the partnership with Frank, buying out his share for £50. From then on his role would be in the garden. No more fine clothes for him; he was condemned to cast-offs. Then she sold the farm at Westbrook to pay off some of the debt and gathered in members of her family to help in repaying the rest. She brought in her sisters, and daughters Ruth and Sylvia (Nancy, the little one, was too young). And to run the XL Stores she summoned their son, Eric, back from Birmingham, where he had been working for a large grocery firm. None of them were to receive any wages until the debt was cleared. As money came in, it was taken straight across the road and paid into the bank.

Eric had been brought up to work hard. The whole family had moved out to their farm at Westbrook for a while in 1919 and Eric, aged 13, had walked the three miles into Hay and done a milk round for his uncle and aunt before going to school. They had Gypsy Castle Farm beyond the church, now a housing estate. But from now on he would have to work exceptionally hard; they all would. The Great Depression was looming and the XL Stores was in competition with many other grocers in the town.

Frank was suicidal at first and told Sarah Ann that he was going to shoot himself. But she said to hold on. Then she went and got his gun and told him to do it at the bottom of the garden so as not to make a mess indoors. At that point she had lost all patience with him.

But she came round, and so did he. He was working in the outdoors that he loved, in the long burgage plots the size of allotments behind the Café Royal and the Wye Hotel. And he was doing the work he had learned as a boy during his apprenticeship at Blenheim Palace. 'He was a fabulous gardener' remembers his granddaughter, Jennifer.

THE 1930S

There was great rejoicing in Hay when the tolls were finally taken off the bridge in 1933. A large crowd gathered on Bridge Street to witness the last toll being taken and the final removal of the gates.

The toll keeper, Mrs Roberts receives the last ever toll before the toll gates at the bottom of Bridge Street came down in 1933. The toll cottage (now demolished) is on the left

By the mid 1930s Bernard Jones, veteran of Mametz Wood, was living at No. 1 Garibaldi Terrace with his wife, the former tailoress Elsie Lewis, and their children. Their eldest son, Ken, would sometimes walk down to visit the family tailoring shop on Broad Street, now run by two of his father's brothers, Ralph and Geoffrey.

London tailoring styles were valued even in remote Hay. His grandfather, Stephen Meredith Jones, had done his apprenticeship in London and sent two of his sons to do the same. Every garment was made to measure and to the customer's individual requirements, which varied widely. Suits for wealthy farmers and the gentry were at one end of the scale; working jackets, waistcoats and trousers at the other. His mother's brother, Uncle Arthur, and two other tailors would be sitting cross-legged on the floor in a room behind the shop, sewing by hand, while Uncle Geoffrey ran the shop. Uncle Ivor's grave was in Hay cemetery and sometimes the young Ken would be taken down to visit it.

Uncle Ralph spent much of his time out in the hills around Hay visiting the farms that provided the bulk of the shop's trade. Armed with measuring tape and large swatches of sample fabrics, he would take orders, then go back a fortnight later to check the fitting of the partially finished garments. It was a form of personalised service that was taken for granted at the time and Ralph Jones was a good salesman, good with people. He and his brother Geoffrey both married and would continue to run the Jones' tailoring business for many years.

Next door but one to the Jones' shop was a bank that had been taken over by Barclays in 1917, and Ken would be sure to walk past it on New Year's Day:

> Every New Year's Day the manager of Barclays Bank would stand on the pavement and give every child who passed a shiny new penny dated for the year that was just beginning. He was known as Dwop Price because his initials were DWOP. He opened the bank on the stroke of nine in the morning by the town clock and at the end of the working day was out on the pavement waiting for the clock to strike again before closing it.

Dwop Price's wife had been a close friend of Katharine Armstrong, and one of the last people to see her before she died.

Life was hard for many in the years following the Great Depression but children enjoyed considerable freedom. 'We had a wonderful childhood', say those who were born and brought up in Hay in the 1920s and '30s. 'It was a magical place.'

Tony Pugh was born in 1924, nephew to the Bill Pugh who opened his sweetshop and tobacconists on the Pavement in 1934:

> There were more open spaces to play in. There were fewer cars on the roads and you could go anywhere.

Hay had always had an open feel to it. Most of the centre had remained undeveloped from Norman times until the seventeenth century, and there were still many pockets of open space left in the 1930s.

The lower end of the millstream had by that time been diverted away from the long triangular pond in which it had once ended. This had been filled in and converted to a garage for the hearse and one or two expensive cars like Mr Birch's Daimler. But the stream itself would continue to flow along the western side of Heol y Dwr all through the 1930s and into the '40s.

The industries on Broad Street's mill site had been vital to the life of the town for over 700 years. The flour used by townspeople for their bread and pies had been milled there; the tannery had produced all their leather. And from the fulling mill had come high-quality flannel for wearing and for trading. By the twentieth century, however, all this was beginning to fall away. The fulling mill ceased to operate in 1907, the tannery went sometime after that, and by 1935 the corn mill was about to go too.

An early twentieth-century photograph of Cadman's at No. 12, Broad Street

A corn and seed merchant/ miller called Frank Cadman was renting the site from Hay Urban District Council at that time, but failing to make it pay. He claimed that the railway company and the council between them were drawing so much water from the millstream that there was not enough left to turn the mill wheel. The flow had been measured at 9,600 gallons an hour back in 1912, so it was not inconsiderable, but Frank Cadman was

The Hay mills finally closed in 1935 but probably looked something like this.
(Photos courtesy of Mr and Mrs Titley, Hundred House Mill)

clear that the mill was no longer viable. 'I have not,' he wrote to the council, 'earned £5 during the past two years'. In 1935 he gave up on the mill altogether and Hay UDC was left with the problem of what to do with the site.

Their answer was to divide it in two. They kept the part furthest from the town, which gave them continued control of the water in the millstream. This enabled them to flush the town sewers, clean the streets and supply the fire engine, whilst also fulfilling their obligation to keep the railway company supplied with the copious quantities used by its steam engines. The greater part of the site was sold off, and was later used for a garage.

Water was, in fact, a problem in the town generally. The domestic supply came from two reservoirs on Hay Common but they were too small to satisfy demand. Bernard Jones's father-in-law, Bill Lewis of No. 2 St Mary's Villas, had helped to dig out the second one by hand in 1895. By the 1930s he was in charge of the stopcock, and on many occasions had to walk round the streets with a handbell warning that the water supply would be shut off at, say, two o'clock to allow levels in the reservoirs to come back up. People would be reduced to collecting water from the Swan Well in big enamel jugs.

Photograph of the millstream, by Alfred Watkins. (Photo courtesy of Hereford Libraries)

Children found the millstream irresistible to play in on their way to and from school. HV's granddaughter, Julie Sinclair, born in 1938, remembers:

> There were lots of yellow flowers like water buttercups. Our aunt in Heol y Dwr used to keep spare shoes and socks for us to change into when they got wet.

Tony Pugh also used to walk to Hay Primary School on Heol y Dwr (where the Police Station is now). He went with Ivor Breeze, who was a good bit younger than him.

> There was an open brook down the side of the road and we used to race floating straws down it from the top. One day Ivor was bending over by the winning post at the bottom when he fell in. I was afraid he'd drown but a great arm came over my shoulder and yanked him out. Mr Mudiman. The Mudimans used to live in The Gardens. They have died out now. [TP]

Ivor's younger brother Bob Breeze and his twin, Betty, had been born on 4 April 1930 in one of the small cottages in The Gardens, off Heol y Dwr. Two years later they would have a younger sister, June. The house was too small for the six of them and in 1932 they moved to West House on Broad Street. Betty Breeze, now Betty Jones, remembers:

> The striking thing is how many children there were compared with now. And there was more of a sense of community. Mrs Wilson, the dentist's wife, used to dress us up in crepe paper for the carnivals. I once had a bonnet with little pleats all round, and my sister was a flag girl, dressed as a flag for Hay's first carnival.

An old saying claims that it takes a whole village to bring up a child, though in this case it was a whole street.

But there was another side to life in the 1930s. The years following the Wall Street Crash of 1929 were hard for working people in ways their children were unaware of. A young man visiting the town in November 1934 wrote:

> Hay, so far from being a cheerful market town of the kind one meets in Worcestershire and, for that matter in Herefordshire also, is very poor. The streets are all narrow and the shops old and dingy. Behind the shopping streets, such as they are, are filthy hovels, unfit for human habitation. The people who walk the streets appear, many of them, to be desperately poor, and the reverse of robust.
>
> It is new to me to see such slum dwellings in rural surroundings such as these but visits to the neighbouring towns of Brecon and Talgarth show them to be every bit as bad and convince me that conditions are the same all over South Wales.[4]

Certainly some of Hay's streets were desperately poor. Chancery Lane (often referred to as Pig Lane) was notorious for its grossly overcrowded cottages and lodging houses (*see p. 51*). Its women were said to be exceptionally tough. Betty and June Breeze would look nervously ahead before venturing up Chancery Lane on their way to school. Frying pans and saucepans flying across the street usually followed any indication of a fight or quarrel going on.

If the lane was clear, they could go straight from there to Hay Primary School, passing Hay Conservative Club, built in 1930, on the way. If not, the alternative route was to go up Heol y Dwr. Either way they would pass the tennis courts and bowling green. The whole area between Chancery Lane and Heol y Dwr would later be taken over by Hay and District Farmers for the mixing and distribution of animal feed, but is now Chancery Court.

Conditions on Chancery Lane might have been squalid, but those on Broad Street were somewhat better. Most of its shops and pubs managed to keep going, although the Seven Stars was de-licensed in 1937. They were helped when the tolls came off the bridge in 1933 and potential customers could come in from Clyro without having to pay to cross the river.

The Three Tuns was one of the pubs most patronised by the men who lived and worked on the street. (It was 'not done' for decent women to frequent drinking establishments.) According to Albert Powell, Mr Wilson, the dentist at No. 25a, would say to his adult male patients, 'Come on boy. Let's go over to the Three Tuns and after that you won't feel a thing'. Tony Pugh was taken to Mr Wilson as a child, however, and he had a different experience. Mr Wilson's wife was kindly and helpful with children, but he himself was less so:

> He was a big fattish man. He'd come towards you with his arms stretched out and all hunched over, like an ogre. I was terrified. He had no children of his own. He used to pump his drill with his foot. His surgery was in the front room with a bay window. Dad took me down there one day and he said to Dad 'You go and leave him with me. He'll be all right.' He sat me up in the dentist's chair and Dad went off. That was about two pm. Five o'clock Dad came back to find me screaming and crying. Wilson had gone off to the Three Tuns and left me. I'd been in that chair all that time. Wilson had forgotten about me and I was too small to venture back up the road by myself. I've had a fear of dentists ever since. I think Dad threatened him over that and Mother took me to a dentist in Hereford. He was impersonal but at least he did the job.

But Dad forgave Mr Wilson and 40 years later went back to him to have all his teeth out. Dad had got rheumatic fever from sleeping on damp ground without a ground sheet in the First World War but Wilson managed to persuade him that it was his teeth making him feel unwell. [TP]

Rock House is third from the left at the top of Ship Pitch (now Newport Street)

The Gas Works

The four Breeze children and their parents moved out of West House in 1937. They went to Rock House at the top of Newport Street where Mrs Breeze was to take on the running of a retail outlet for the Hay Gas and Coke Company,[5] selling gas stoves and gas fires from the two front rooms of the house. Betty Jones, née Breeze, remembers her mother selling the chalky white bars called radiants that diffused the heat from the gas fires, and the mantles for domestic gas lamps. Most houses were lit by gas at that time, though often only on the ground floor. A ring on the end of a chain was pulled to release the gas, and the mantle sprang to life with a loud pop at the application of a lighted taper. Bedrooms were, in general, still lit only by candles.

Betty (on the right) with her sister, June, in a photo from 1936, the year of the coronation of George VI. Gas stoves can be seen behind them in the shop, and their mother is just visible. (Photo courtesy of Betty Jones)

The Hay Gas Works on their sunken site at the bottom of Newport Street. The house facing the railway line was occupied by a Mr and Mrs Barber who sold Calor gas cylinders while trains passed directly above

But the place that fascinated the children most was the gas works where their father, Bert Breeze, was manager. Six men worked there, shovelling coal into five huge, specialised furnaces called retorts, each about 15 feet (4.6m) long. Outside was an engine room for pumping the gas that came off the coal into two large gas-holders that would rise higher and higher until they were full:

> Then they would open the big iron doors of the retorts and throw cold water on the glowing bright red coke inside. It made a great hissing and clouds of steam. We used to love to go and watch that happening when we were children. [BJ]

Eric Pugh, son of Bill Pugh, once made a film of Bert Breeze shovelling coal into the retorts and the clouds of steam coming off when the water was poured. He and a friend took it down to the Gas Board in Newport where it aroused much interest, but it got lent to Cardiff University and has never been seen since. The Gas Board may have been particularly interested in the film because the retorts were of some considerable historical importance, being virtually the same as those used in the country's first commercial coal gas plant back in 1808.[6] They would remain in use in Hay until the gas works finally became redundant in the 1970s, by which time they were among the last of their kind.

The tramway had run conveniently above the sunken gas works site, enabling coal to be tipped from the wagons straight down into its yard, but when trains replaced the tramway the coal had to be transported from the station. In the 1930s it was a Mr Reg Morgan who repeatedly filled his horse-drawn cart with coal at the station yard, drove the few hundred yards to a low wall, and tipped it down into the gas works yard.

> That horse and cart was used for all kinds of other things as well, like moving household furniture. Mr Morgan lived down the Brecon Road. When the coke was cold some of it was taken out of the retorts and slung into the corner. Later the coke was shovelled into sacks and sold to local people for burning with coal. Either people would come down to the gas works to buy the coke or Mr Morgan would deliver it with his horse and cart. [BJ]

The ovens in the Hitchcox bakery were fired with coke. Mr Morgan would call at the Café Royal every day and speak to Sarah Ann:

> How are you fixed today, mum?
> We're alright for today, Mr Morgan, but we could do with a load for tomorrow.
> Right you are, mum.
>
> NEIL HITCHCOX

And when tomorrow came he would back his horse and cart down the entryway beside the XL Stores and tip the coke into the coke house adjacent to the bakery.

> Coal tar was a by-product. That went into big tin barrels that were collected by a lorry. And another by-product from the process was a yellowish powder they called 'oxide'. This was kept in one of the sheds to the right of the door from Cats Park.[7] Kids would be sent down to lean over it and deeply breathe in the fumes from it if they had breathing difficulties like asthma.
>
> BETTY JONES

People now in their 80s and 90s, who were sent down to breathe in the oxide fumes as children, say the effect was instantaneous. Blocked sinuses and bronchial passages would clear instantly. The fumes smelt like tar.

> The site had a railing all the way round it with one gate on Wyeford Road, pretty much where those ornamental iron gates are now, and a door on Cats Park. The railings were taken down in the war and melted down for scrap metal to make armaments. [BJ]

The six men employed were responsible for the gas works themselves, but also for laying the gas mains under the roads and repairing leaks. The mains were dug manually. There were no mechanical diggers in the 1930s.

The sunken site was subject to flooding and on two occasions the Wye rose high enough to extinguish the retorts. The first of these was in 1852 when the retorts were cracked, but there was almost no damage in March

1963, when the snow melted after a long winter. The holders had been full, the retorts were only out for one day and no one went without gas.

> In the 1970s [between 1967 and 1977] North Sea Gas was brought in down the railway line and the gas works were finished. Dad bought the whole site and sold it for bungalows to be built. [BJ]

Today, the site of the former gas works has been raised to road level and is occupied by bungalows.

The Second World War

The Second World War came much closer to Hay than the First had done. Men had gone away to war the first time round, and women had gone to work in the munitions factory at Rotherwas, but that was about as close as it got. The second time was very different. Soldiers were posted in the town, military vehicles lined the lanes, and evacuees came in from the big cities. The town was not even exempt from the risk of bombing. German aircrew would jettison the last of their bombs over the Black Mountains as they flew back to Germany after a night raid on the Midlands, and one fell on nearby Llanigon. Traffic had to be diverted round the back lanes for weeks.

Bert Breeze was in the Royal Observer Corps and would track approaching planes from an underground cell in a field high up on the other side of the Wye. He would then sound the air raid warning. And as the ominous sound travelled over the valley, his wife and children would hurry down into the cellar of Rock House, which they used in lieu of an air raid shelter.

But the biggest explosion in the area was not from the bomb that fell on Llanigon. It was from an ammunition dump near the walled garden at Gwernyfed, five miles out of Hay. Something went wrong there and the whole lot went up in one of the biggest explosions of the war. Schoolboys would pick up grenades, anti-tank rockets, rifle ammo and all sorts of things for years after the war had ended. One wall of the garden was damaged and is still breeze-blocked today.

Most of the large houses round Hay were requisitioned by the military.

At The Moor, then just outside Hay on the Bredwardine Road but now demolished, there was a large contingent of American soldiers and the estate became a camp with sheds and Nissen huts lining the drive. At first these housed Italian prisoners-of-war, though they were later transferred to Nissen huts on land beside the sawmill on Potter's Lane (Nantyglasdwr Lane) owned by Bill and Florrie Potter.

The middle section of the old Tanners Arms was by now a fish and chip shop, the only one in town. It was run by Martin Jones and his wife (grandparents to David Jones, the accountant), and sold 'terrific fish and chips' that were popular with soldiers, evacuees and locals alike. It was the only food that could be got without ration coupons, and the queue would often stretch right down Broad Street. American soldiers would get their fish and chips wrapped in newspaper, then tramp back across the fields with them singing 'We don' wanna go back to the Moor no more'.

Girls would try and congregate in the Café Royal to wait for the soldiers, but Sarah Ann would have none of it. She would tell one of the girls who worked for her to 'go in there and clear them out.' And if they were a bit tough-looking and the girl was too frightened to approach them, Sarah Ann would go in and clear them out herself.

This was the first time that most of Hay's population had seen people with skin of a different colour. A large contingent of Indian soldiers coming through on horseback was an exciting sight for some, whilst others were frightened. Julysia Webb, born 1938, was the daughter of Humphrey Webb and granddaughter to HV. She couldn't believe her eyes when confronted by her first African Americans, having had no idea that there were people in the world who looked so different from those she knew. Mesmerised by their unfamiliar music, she would press her ear to the thin partition dividing No. 3 from the back bar of the Three Tuns and listen as they sang 'Swing Low Sweet Chariot' and other songs of the American South. She learned the words by heart and would try to pick out the tunes on the family piano.

On the opposite corner of Bridge Street, evacuees from London were running the Black Swan and more evacuees occupied the now disused toll house on Bridge Street. There were so many evacuee children sent away from heavily bombed city areas that extra schoolrooms had to be provided, one of them in the basement of the Ebeneezer Chapel on Broad Street (now

The Globe). Some of the children liked living in Hay and some didn't. Some were affronted by the way that milk was delivered by being ladled into a jug at the front door. Proper milk, they thought, came in bottles.

Sarah Ann's son, Eric, was running the XL Stores with his wife. When he received his call-up papers Florrie Potter pointed out that he was supplying both the Moor and Gwernyfed with groceries, and so could apply for reserved occupation. He said he'd accepted the need to go but Florrie insisted that he had no need and in the end he didn't. His son, Neil, remembers:

> My parents were kept very busy in the shop as food rationing made everything more complicated. Besides most things having to be weighed and packed, customers were only able to have what their ration books allowed. When supplies became short people were only allowed 2ozs of butter per person per week. So there was no need for diets. At one point Dad found himself with more rationed provisions than he could legally disperse. Some of the market traders who came on a Thursday took them to sell in South Wales but were caught on the way down by a food inspector called Matthias. When the food was traced back to Dad he was fined £50.
>
> NEIL HITCHCOX

During his holidays Neil used to help his grandmother, Sarah Ann, prepare sandwiches in the café:

> We would start off with long sandwich loaves which my father would slice on his bacon machine on the Wednesday evening and leave wrapped up in cloth. Then all the bacon and ham ends from the grocery shop would be boiled up. On Thursday morning these would be minced up with a good helping of mustard and pepper and salt mixed in. Margarine was used on the bread. Grandma used to say 'Spread it on and scrape it off and make sure there's plenty of salt.' Half a pound of cooking margarine went a long way and after all the salt the market dealers and country folk would be drinking tea from the café all day long.

> Up until the end of World War Two lunches cost 1/- with 6d extra for a pudding. Many of the farmers would spend their time in the pubs and it was not unknown for some of them to get into the trap so drunk that the horse had to find its own way home. [NH]

Sarah Ann was generous in feeding people who were in need, and there were a lot of them. The queue of those waiting for the Labour Exchange on the Pavement to open would often stretch right back down Broad Street. People would often knock on the door at night or go into the shop at the end of the day to be given stale cakes and buns, or left over rice pudding.

> An old lady called Miss Philips who lived right over the top of the Black Mountains would come in sometimes to help Grandma clear up at the end of the day. She'd bring a big strong basket and Grandma would help her load it with left-over food to take home. Dad too would dispense out-of-date things from the grocery. [NH]

> Farmers' wives would bring round covered baskets full of stuff to sell during the war. Under the cover was stuff that should perhaps have been declared. The black market. They used to sell a lot of boiler chickens. These were old chickens that had stopped laying and were tough. Very good with parsley sauce once they had been boiled up for a long time though.
>
> Julie Sinclair, née Julysia Webb

The turning point of the war was D-day, 6 June 1944. This was the day of the Normandy landings that began the liberation of German-occupied France and laid the foundations of the Allied victory on the Western Front. It was an enormous operation, the largest seaborne invasion in history, and involved tens of thousands of vehicles. Lorries came in steadily from America for 18 months beforehand and were parked on smaller roads all over the country, camouflaged so that the Germans couldn't see them from the air. Even roads as far from the coast as those around Hay were used as lorry parks. The back roads to Talgarth and either side of the Moor Estate were jammed with American lorries that disappeared overnight in a mass exodus as D-day approached.

Men from the street who were involved in fighting in the Second World War included Roger Golesworthy. His grandfather had opened the outfitter's shop on the corner of Lion Street and Broad Street in the late 1800s, and by now the business had expanded into the two shops previously occupied by Stephen Jones, the tailor. Roger became a signalman in the Royal Corps of Signals and served in India and Burma. In the foothills of northern India he saw scenes of utter devastation as the Japanese army retreated.

> The army went straight into the attack against the now-retreating Japanese hordes. Three men were used to drive the truck – one steering, one changing gear and one operating the clutch as they drove over the cardboard cut-out flattened bodies of the destroyed Indian National Army and their Japanese masters. The hillsides were littered with corpses, a charnel house straight out of Dante's *Inferno* with huge vultures enjoying a culinary delight. One of these birds decided to launch itself from one hillside to inspect the opposite one. Pity about the truck! Hitting the windscreen support it disassembled itself into blood, gore, feathers and talons straight onto the heads of all three drivers.[8]

From India, Roger was sent to Rangoon, Burma and he was there when the war ended. It was on the ship coming home that he met the woman he would marry. Anna Valk, from the Dutch East Indies, had just been released from a Japanese concentration camp and was being repatriated to Amsterdam with nothing but the clothes she stood up in. He gave her his battledress to use as a coat, the pair became inseparable, and by the time the ship reached Alexandria in Egypt they were engaged to be married.

Roger was sent to Bletchley Park when the ship reached England, but Anna headed for Hay where she was met at the train station by Roger's father, Arthur Golesworthy. He never forgot that first sight of her. The steam cleared, he would say later, and there she was.[9] He was short, as were most people in Hay at that time, but she was tall and, he said, the most beautiful woman he had ever seen, in a picture hat and a pair of army boots. She would become his daughter-in-law.

8

Rampaging Cows and a Fourth Bridge

After the Second World War

Victory in Europe day, 5 May 1945, was marked with wild celebrations on Broad Street. There was dancing in the street to live music by the two blind Keylock brothers who were set up on a makeshift stage under the clock tower playing piano, saxophone and whatever else came to their talented hands.

> Barrels of tar were set alight after dark and rolled down Belmont Road, the flaming tar spurting everywhere, running down the drains. Thunder Flashers, used in training during the war, went off with huge bangs. Pillows and mattresses were split open and feathers showered everywhere. It made a helluva mess, people were just going wild and the police thought it best to just let them get on with it, get it out of their systems.
>
> Neil Hitchcox

Tony Pugh had flown as rear gunner in Lancaster bombers and would probably have stayed in the RAF afterwards if his mother hadn't written to say that his father was poorly. Their fish, fruit and vegetable shop on Lion Street would have to close, she wrote, unless he came home to help run it, so he came back to Hay and was always glad that he did.

Officers of Bernard Jones's former regiment, the 38th Borderers, had been stationed at the Crown Hotel during the war. Tony Pugh's memories of the Crown after the war are vivid:

> The Crown was a brilliant place. It was in a rough condition after the soldiers had been stationed there but at the end of the war it was bought by a man from Switzerland. He was called Guller and he spent a lot of money on it. When it reopened it was one of the loveliest hotels you could imagine.
>
> The dining room was on the ground floor where the Old Electric Shop is now. You'd get 30 or 40 people at a long table. Wonderful parties! One Christmas Eve there was a dinner party with food we hadn't seen all through the war. There was cream this and cream that. I don't know where he got it. We never asked. [NH]

Nissen huts left over from the war had been used by Mr Guller to construct a ballroom in the yard at the back of the hotel where the livery stables had once been, and the dances there were very popular.

> My cousin Joyce was a wonderful girl, very nice looking. I was very proud of her. When we went to dances at the Crown friends would nudge me and say 'Is that your cousin? Can you get me a dance with her?' and I'd say 'You get your own dances with her!'
>
> TONY PUGH

An advert for the Crown in the late 1940s describes it as the leading hotel in the town, with catering facilities for 250 people, hot and cold water in all bedrooms, central heating, a new cocktail bar and excellent cuisine.

Sarah Ann Hitchcox had slowed down considerably by the time the war was over. She might even sit down for a quarter of an hour with one of her staff. 'Now girl' she would say to Valerie Wilding, 'let's have a cup of tea and a bun'.

But a lifetime of exceptionally hard work and the habit of never spending a penny on herself had paid off. In 1946 she felt able to retire altogether. She was 73. She had not only settled Frank's debt but had saved enough to buy him and herself a house on Oxford Road, ensure that each of their four children could be provided with a house and a business, and look after some of her sisters.

Frank would die in September 1953 but Sarah Ann lived on to July 1967 and the age of 94, indomitable to the end. Her generous spirit is typified by an incident from the 1930s when two drunks appeared at the Westbrook family farm demanding cider with menaces. Her brother, Tom Lane, had a gammy leg and they easily managed to knock him down, but Sarah Ann went for them with the yard broom and managed to hold them off until the

Eric Hitchcox standing outside the Café Royal, with the tea room that was formerly the XL Stores in the background. (Photo courtesy of Neil Hitchcox)

police arrived. When she discovered later that they had ended up in prison, however, leaving their families in danger of destitution, she sent food to the families for the duration. She is buried with Frank in Winforton churchyard.

The Café Royal became home to Eric and his family when Sarah Ann retired, while the Wye Hotel went to her eldest daughter, Sylvia. Eric had long been running the XL Stores, housed in the former post office building, but now he was in charge of the whole Broad Street operation. There was no more sitting down with a cup of tea and a bun for Valerie Wilding. Eric was a taskmaster, with steel tips on his heels so you could hear him coming. 'Is everyone working hard here?' No meal breaks at all.

His eldest son, Graham, wanted to be a farmer, his attachment to the land having been formed on the family farm at Winforton, but Eric needed him on Broad Street. With Graham's help he moved the grocery shop out of the post office building and into the front room of the Café Royal, where he had long mahogany counters installed down either side. It was the classic grocery shop design of the time. A similar layout can be seen today at St Fagan's Museum outside Cardiff.

The former grocery in the old post office next door became a tea room with a gas fire; a place where farmers could feel at ease in their muddy boots while their wives went into the back room of the Café Royal with its well-polished linoleum floor and coal fire. The dining room on the first floor was more up-market still. A three-course lunch here cost 4/6d with coffee 6d extra.

There were still nothing like enough seats to meet the demand for meals on Thursdays however. The expectation back in 1919, that trade would drop when the cattle market left Broad Street, had not been realised. Market stalls now stretched the length of the road on market days, and the cobbled pavement opposite would also be brought into use. People would pour into town from all over, and bus-loads would be deposited by the clock tower. A long queue would form outside the door of the Café Royal, and as seats became free Eric would raise the security bar across the door and allow a few more in. Local people were refused service on market days to make room for those who came from out of town.

THE COBBLED PAVEMENT MARKET

It was usually left to the women of the local farms to raise the money for those food items that could not be produced on the farms themselves, tea, sugar, salt and flour. On Thursday mornings therefore, market day, they would bring in to Broad Street whatever they had managed to gather for sale that week.

There might be whimberries from the mountainside, or wild mushrooms; primroses and violets came from the hedgerows, herbs and rhubarb from their gardens. Produce from their farms included hand-churned butter, or cheese, and eggs from ducks, geese, chickens and guinea fowl. A goose wing pressed into a fan made an effective brush for sweeping and loose feathers went for stuffing pillows as long as they were dry. Outside West House there was frequently a pole hung with rabbits for sale.

For the sale of things like eggs, the farm women would often go straight to local housewives they knew, or otherwise to the traders from the Welsh valleys they called hucksters. But to display goods without going to the cost of hiring a market stall the raised cobbled pavement on the south side of Broad Street was used. Women had no doubt done the same thing in Norman times and it would continue into the 1960s.

When the Black Swan next door was put up for sale then, Eric promptly snapped it up. Run by evacuees during the war, it had become known as the Mucky Duck and was de-licensed in 1946, whereupon its value dropped overnight from something approaching £2,000 to a mere £600. Eric's idea was to extend the café into it, and he even had plans drawn up for the conversion. When the cost of this was estimated at £50, however, he had second thoughts. Always reluctant to spend money on alterations or repairs to property, he splashed out £1,100 on a Rover 75 car instead and the plans were never put into operation. The Black Swan was rented out.

Geoff and Amy Price would become its tenants in 1953 at five shillings a week and would remain there for many years. Eric paid the rates in return for Geoff, who was a jobbing builder, doing any work that needed doing. His workshop was in the old stables in the back yard, which have now been converted to residential use.

The winter of 1947 was exceptionally cold:

> There was snow everywhere and farmers couldn't get their trucks out because of it. I remember the animals had to walk in to market from Clifford and all over. The stock all got mixed up and it was chaos.
>
> Farmer at Hay cattle market

Chimney fires would occur quite frequently at the Café Royal as coal was banked up high. The fire engine was called out regularly. Oak lintels above fireplaces would sometimes smoulder unnoticed for months as the beam slowly burned through from the back.

The warmest place was the bakery. This was small, measuring something like 50 feet by 20 (15m x 6m), and the coke-fired ovens took up a good deal of the space; but it managed to produce huge quantities of baked goods nonetheless. Bread was still rationed in the early 1950s along with sweets, but most families continued to buy their bread instead of either making it, or having it made for them, at home. The domestic servants of the pre-war period had all but disappeared.

Rationing ended in 1954 but money was still short and meals in the Café Royal were kept very simple to keep the price down. Those who could not afford whole biscuits could get a bag of broken ones for a penny, and Eric was fond of saying that the shop was sometimes so strapped for cash he was glad to get that penny. Prosperity gradually increased, however, and by the end of the decade the Hitchcox bakery was busier than ever. Its full-time baker, Mr Coles, was assisted by a young apprentice called Dai Ratcliffe.

> They baked bread, buns, doughnuts, fancy cakes, swiss rolls and fruit cakes. Also wedding cakes. At Christmas time there would be two bakers working flat out making Christmas cakes and Yule logs plus all the other Christmas varieties. Dai Ratcliffe told me that one Christmas broke all previous records when a thousand dozen mince pies were made.

Christmas morning was the bakers' perk. People would bring their chickens, turkeys and geese to be cooked in the ovens, for which the baker would charge 10/- that he was allowed to keep. We supplied the fuel for the fires.

At one time there were three main bakehouses in the town, Maddys, Stevens and ours, though there was also Potty Watkins on that corner of Lion Street where it makes the right-angled turn. He was still baking bread in the old-fashioned way with a fire lit inside the oven itself and raked out once the oven was hot enough so that the bread could go in. This to my memory was the best bread of all.

Neil Hitchcox

Potty Watkins lived at No. 28 Broad Street in one of the three cottages set back from the Tanners Arms. Married to one of Tony Pugh's aunts, their daughter was his cousin, Joyce, who was so popular at the Crown dances.

Tony Pugh remembers:

> He was called Potty because he was eccentric. He wore a filthy black stained apron from raking out the ashes of the fire in the oven but baked the loveliest cakes and buns you'd ever expect to get. It was rumoured that he never paid any tax and left a fortune buried in the wall of the bakery when he died. I don't know if the man who bought the bakery later ever found the money.

The Hitchcox's baker, Mr Coles, had a few eccentricities of his own.

> We used to call him Old King Cole and he was mad as a hatter. He had a ferocious temper on him and he would go beserk, chucking 10lb weights at Dai Ratcliffe.

Neil Hitchcox

He may have had a temper on him but Mr Coles was well respected as a healer and was much in demand by farmers with bad backs. He cured Irene Webb's leg ulcers and could even get rid of warts. Humphrey Webb ran a taxi service alongside the other Webb enterprises, and he would take Mr

Coles into Hereford to get the supplies he needed for his healing work from Heath and Heather, the 1950s version of Holland and Barratt.

> Dad went into the bakehouse one day to find a young female member of staff sitting on the bottom step of the flight up to the flour loft with Mr Coles kneeling in front of her. His hands were on her leg. Dad was outraged. 'What on earth's going on here?' But it was just that she had twisted her ankle or something and Mr Coles was trying to put it right for her.
>
> NEIL HITCHCOX

The problem for the Hitchcoxes was that the healing activities of Mr Coles tended to take precedence over his work as a baker.

> The day came when he took off on some healing mission or other without telling anyone and left an oven full of wedding cakes to burn. That day was his last. Father got rid of him after that. Dai Ratcliffe took over as chief baker and that was the end of Old King Cole. [NH]

Today there are still three bakers in town – though, perhaps regrettably, none of them use the Potty Watkins method of lighting a fire inside the oven. Mr Coles's healing hands are long gone but Health Matters in the old Boardroom on Broad Street offers a range of complementary therapies.

Dai Ratcliffe would go on to run a bakery of his own on Castle Street with his wife Mary – and, at various different times, the Swan Hotel at the far end of town, and the Seven Stars on Broad Street. Before finally retiring, Dai ran a fish and chip shop in the old post office building on Broad Street. Fish and chips can still be bought there today, though it is now called Hay Takeaway.

The Webbs

Four-year-old Julysia Webb was living in No. 3, Old House, when she put her ear to the partition and heard the American soldiers singing in the Three Tuns, and it would remain her home throughout her childhood. But it was also a shop. While her father ran the Webb garage on Lion street, her mother, Irene, supplied a whole range of goods and services connected with cars, bikes, radio batteries and home hardware. She worked from No. 3 itself, the alleyway beside it, and the shop beyond that. Even the pavement alongside the road was brought into use.

Today that alleyway has been integrated into a building, like many of those on Broad Street that once gave access to the former burgage plots behind. It now forms part of the Hourglass shop.

Irene Webb had been born Irene Bryan. Her mother had been working at the Crown during the Armstrong affair, and told her the story of how she had met the Scotland Yard detectives who climbed to the top of the clock tower to watch Armstrong's comings and goings. Irene had become a Webb by marrying Humphrey, the youngest of HV's 13 children.

The childhood memories of her daughter Julysia (now Julie Sinclair) remain vivid:

> Inside the front door of No. 3 you had to go down some steps into the hallway and at the back of this was a large table. On it was a machine for charging radio batteries and at any one time a number of batteries would stand there being charged. They were the old-fashioned glass type with a metal carrying handle. New battery acid had to be poured into them before they could be re-charged and my mother's overalls always had holes in them where the acid had splashed. This is before the outlying farms around Hay had electricity.

Irene Webb beside the petrol pump on the pavement outside her shop. The alleyway with the second pump is directly behind her. (Photo courtesy of Julie Sinclair)

On the right-hand side of No. 3's front door was a shop where Irene Webb sold bicycles and motorbikes, though customer access to it was from the alleyway. Motorbikes were displayed on the pavement, but locked into the alleyway at night. Another branch of the Webb family had once had a bicycle shop on Lion Street but that had closed by this time.

There were two petrol pumps – one selling Regular grade, and one Premium. HV had installed an early form of pump on the narrow pavement outside No. 3 in the early 1920s but this had by now been replaced with an electric one.

> There was a second pump in the alleyway. Customers had to go round it to get to the door of the bicycle shop. The petrol had to be pumped up by hand and to operate it Mum had to get up some steps. [JS]

Then further down the alleyway were drums of paraffin with dippers for filling the cans brought in by customers.

> As a child I helped with doing this and it was a messy job. The paraffin was used for the oil heaters people had in their homes. And there were cabinets with engine oil, sold by the pint or half pints. You pulled a handle down and the oil came out. [JS]

Cattle in Broad Street

The alleyway was useful as a well-ventilated place from which to serve petrol, oil and paraffin, as well as for keeping motorbikes locked up overnight. But it was a source of potential trouble whenever a consignment of cows came over the bridge on their way to the slaughterhouse. The iron bridge built by Thomas Savin had never been very strong and by the 1950s its weight limit had been reduced to two-and-a-half tons. Vehicles above that weight, including lorries bringing animals for slaughter, had to stop on the far side of the bridge and all the animals, cows, sheep and pigs, were driven across. But the danger to the Webb's alleyway came mainly from the cows.

> As they got near to the end of the bridge the cows seemed to somehow smell the blood from the slaughterhouse and they would go berserk, rampaging around. There was one time when a cow went charging down our alleyway and it was difficult to get it out again. So the cry would go up 'Cows coming' and there would be a rush to get to the gates that were kept down the alleyway and lift them back into place across the entrance. They were head height and padlocked at night.
>
> Julie Sinclair

The slaughterhouse was behind Mr Kedward's former shop at No. 8, built by a butcher called Harry Lewis, who had moved there from St John's Place and built the slaughterhouse at the back. By the 1950s, however, shop and slaughterhouse were being run by his niece, Nellie Lewis, and her assistant Bill the Butcher, who was also the slaughterman.

> We used to go swimming in the river quite a bit, over the other side but blood from the slaughterhouse would all run down into the river, it was a regular thing to see it there. When we saw the blood coming we got out quick. We stopped swimming there anyway once the polio epidemic took hold. [JS]

> Blood in the river used to cause great shoals of perch and chubb to gather. You could look down from the bridge and see them.
>
> Neil Hitchcox

SLAUGHTERHOUSES

Small slaughterhouses would be phased out over the years in favour of larger and more regulated abattoirs, but there were once at least three in Hay. They dealt with all kinds of animals; bulls and bullocks, cows, sheep, chickens and pigs, and each type of animal had a killing method devised specifically for it.

Slaughtermen would also go out to farms in the locality when needed, and to those households in the town that still kept a pig. Pig keeping was a form of urban self-sufficiency that had been practised since Norman times and would not finally die out until the 1960s.

> When we lived at Garibaldi Terrace Dad used to keep a pig or two in the orchard at the back. We'd feed them up, apples and scraps and that. Bill the Butcher who worked for Nellie Lewis would come up and kill them. We used to hang the carcasses in the shed up there.
>
> KEN JONES

Those who wanted to keep a pig or two but did not have an orchard or a suitable garden could often find a place to keep them in the area between the end of the Heol y Dwr gardens and the town wall. This is now occupied by a small housing estate called Booth Gardens but at various times over the years has held both pigs and the town allotments. It was probably used for keeping animals from the outset. The Liberal Club was also there at one time, as was Henderson's factory making machine parts.

Beyond the Webb's alleyway was the other half of Irene Webb's shop. Here you could buy china and crockery, wallpaper and a host of other things. A large stock of wallpaper was kept in the attic of No. 3, and Julysia was warned off from playing with it in the phrase aimed at children everywhere – *Don't you go touching that now.*

Next came Mr Vale, the saddler, who had a lock-up shop with a workshop behind. His wife, Taddy, was one of Sarah Ann Hitchcox's sisters. The tannery had closed by this time but Mr Vale continued the centuries-old tradition of making and repairing leather goods on Broad Street nonetheless. His leather shop at the front had very high counters with divided trays on them for nails and so on. His workshop was down some steps at the back.

> I used to go in and watch him and help a bit when I was small. He made my first school satchel and leather music case and that music case is still in use in the family today. I used to call them Uncle and Auntie Vale. She was a little woman. He was quite a big man with a stomach on him, very skilled, used to repair all the footballs for Hay St Mary's. They had one son, Laddie Vale, who died having polyps removed from his nose. He'd been in the Camel Corps in somewhere like Egypt or the Sudan.
>
> JULIE SINCLAIR

After Mr Vale's came another alleyway, whose position is marked today by a stone lintel, and everything beyond that has now been demolished to make way for the Mill Bank housing estate. Formerly, however, there was a house with a bay window on the first floor and then the mill site.

The site of the former Hay mills had been a large one, covering an area that sloped downhill from the road to the top of the riverbank. It had been divided in 1935, with Hay UDC keeping the part furthest from the centre of town for the sake of its water supply. By the late 1940s, however, alternative provision had been made and the millpond, now cut off from running water, had become stagnant and filthy. Children were warned not to go near it, and a high wall with boarded insets was erected between it and the road. Old cars were dumped at the bottom of that part of the site, and George Keylock, who went round the country selling army surplus, parked his bus there. Chickens scratched around in the dust and there were chicken sheds.

But the greater part of the old mill site was bought by a man called Spencer Hall, who used it to open a garage. Around 1948 he moved his family into the house with the bay window, and proceeded to form a repair workshop out of the old tannery running down the side of the site. One of the old mill buildings became a showroom for new cars, and he installed a petrol pump on the pavement outside. Car ownership must have increased to the point where he felt this was needed, because the Webbs already had two pumps a few yards away.

He was always well-dressed and, perhaps unusually for a man who ran a garage, not keen on getting his hands dirty. Tony Pugh remembers:

> There was Webb's garage and then Hall's. Both had a petrol pump outside. Spencer Hall, well I could write a book about him. He had three children. It was a big garage, ran down the slope so far you could put three buses there. One day my Dad pulled in there and asked for two gallons please. Spencer Hall was pulling on his gloves. He shouted to one of his mechanics, who was working under a bus at the far end to leave that and come and serve some petrol. Dad was disgusted. He said 'You can keep your petrol if you're too lazy to serve it yourself' and drove off.

Albert Powell had been born in 1922, the year that his parents took over the Three Tuns, and he worked on the buses for a time.

> The buses were kept there. I was a bus driver for a while. I did alternate shifts with Fred Crook, Bobby Crook's father. We would leave Hay at eight in the morning, go to Glasbury, pick up a lot of people in Talgarth and take them all on to Brecon where they worked. Some of them were in the Inland Revenue there, or other government departments, or shops. There weren't so many cars in those days and the buses were used a lot. It was the Wales and West Bus Company. The buses were single-deckers. Each one had a driver and a conductor. I started as a conductor but went on to become a driver. This was after the war. The buses were kept in Spencer Hall's garage overnight. The entrance from Broad Street was very narrow and it was very difficult to get them in and out. Sometimes we would be trying to get a bus in at gone eleven at night. The conductor would have to get out and help. They'd be shouting 'Back up, back up, Stop! Stop! Move back'. It was very difficult. Later the buses were kept at Like's garage where there was more room. We had the key to lock the gates at night. [TP]

Mr Vale died in 1953 or '54, shortly after making Julysia Webb's brother a leather satchel. His lock-up shop, workshop and the yard at the far back were all taken over by Humphrey Webb, who found good uses for them as part of the undertaking business he had taken on from his father. Mr Vale's former workshop was converted into a Chapel of Rest. Coffins had to be carried along the alleyway and down a few steps to get into it, but it was peaceful and secluded. The yard at the back became a mason's yard.

> A man called Charles Williams worked as a stonemason in Cusop but asked Dad if he would be interested in taking him on to deal with the gravestones. So the yard at the back became the mason's yard and our coal and woodshed became Charlie's workshop. He would do all the lettering on the stones, sometimes painting them black, or adding gold leaf, or hammering in letters made of lead. Then he would also erect the stones in the graveyard.
>
> JULIE SINCLAIR

The entire undertaking business was now being run from Broad Street, apart from the making of the coffins. This was still done in the Webbs' garage on Lion Street, where Humphrey lost the top of one finger on the planing machine, which had no guard.

Mr Vale's former shop became a car showroom, the second one on Broad Street.

> It was only big enough for one car but it provided a shop window for the car sales business that was run from the Lion Street garage. For a window dressing competition run by the Hay Chamber of Trade, Dad borrowed Mr Birch's Daimler to put in there and did it all up as a country scene with stuffed game birds and heather and all. [JS]

The car showroom would later become Pinocchio's Italian restaurant, but is now the Pinewood Health and Beauty Studio.

In 1957 work began on another new bridge for Hay. The original one of 1793 had had five stone arches, partially replaced by wood after a storm. Thomas Savin's had been of iron. The new one would have twin pillars of concrete and be constructed to the side of Savin's, leaving the houses on Bridge Street in a straight line while the road had to bend slightly away.

Its completion in 1958 meant the weight limit so necessary for Savin's bridge could be lifted at last. Lorries could cross, including those bringing animals to the slaughterhouse on Broad Street. The Webb's alleyway ran no further risk of invasion by rampaging cows.

9

Richard Booth Creates a Booktown

THE Swinging Sixties ushered in the beginning of a new era for Hay. The austerity of the post-war period was over, new people arrived, new businesses opened, and one of Sarah Ann's grandsons was in a rock and roll band. A long process of renovation began on the fabric of the town and, surprisingly at first, second-hand bookshops began to appear.

But it was also a decade of loss. The 1960s saw the end of both the gas works and the much-valued railway.

The End of the Railway

Hay's railway closed even before the infamous Beeching Report of March 1963 recommended closing nearly 40% of Britain's branch lines. The last train left Hay Station on Saturday 29 December 1962 bound for Hereford, and stationmaster, Mr Maurice John, retired at more or less the same time. He would continue to live in the last house on Bridge Street, bought by the railway to house its stationmasters, but from now on he would spend more time working on his allotment below the level of the bridge on the other side of the road. Today it is part of the picnic area.

The loss of the Hay railway was much lamented at the time, and is still regretted today. It had been a convenient way to get to Hereford in one direction and Brecon in the other, though it had never really paid its way. Only four passenger trains a day ran in each direction and by the beginning of the 1960s road transport was increasingly taking over the delivery of coal and other goods. Closure had become inevitable.

The remains of Hay railway station, in a state of dereliction

The station site was taken over by Hay and Brecon Farmers, the brick engine shed used for their giant sacks of animal feed. The railway track was taken up and its route became 'the old railway line', now a broad woodland path above the river.

And the Gas Works

From Boxing Day 1962 onwards the weather had been exceptionally harsh and the river had frozen over. Robert Golesworthy was nine. His father, Roger, let him and his brother stand on ice flows in the river and paddle themselves along with poles. Tony Pugh's brother, who would later become a British ambassador, was pulled along over the ice by a Great Dane.

The gas works were flooded once the thaw set in, though supply was not disrupted. In 1965, however, the town was connected to the national grid and the gas works followed its railway into oblivion.[1] The sunken site on which they had stood was built up to road level and is today occupied by bungalows.

A Second-hand Bookshop

But 1962, the year the railway closed, was also the year that saw the opening of Hay's first second-hand bookshop, an experiment that would eventually lead to the town's transformation. At the time, however, it was an open question whether or not there was a market for used books in this remote, rural market town. Most people who thought about it at all, thought not. But Mrs Dworski from Clyro, wife of the potter Adam Dworski, went searching through the shelves and found something to buy, and she was among the first of the many thousands who would follow. For the shop was owned by Richard George William Pitt Booth, later to become the self-styled King of Hay and tireless promoter of a new phenomenon known as the 'booktown'.

Hay's first bookshop was in the old fire station on Castle Street. Later, and for many years, it would be Boz Books and it is now the Ty Tan Art gallery. Mrs Joan Hamilton of No. 22 Broad Street managed it for Richard Booth as he himself was spending much of his time on the road, gathering up books from disbanded libraries, much as John Leland had done 300 years before. Unlike Leland, however, he was collecting from country houses[2] rather than monasteries and sending the books not to London, but to Hay. And in huge quantities. Far more than one small shop could contain. The sheds and outbuildings of the Booth family home at Brynmelyn, Cusop Dingle, were soon filled to capacity.

Wigington Antiques

It was not long then before he was looking at Hay Castle as a repository for some of the thousands of books he was bringing into the town. It was empty and up for sale at an asking price of £5,500. But there were other potential buyers. Colin and Bryan Wigington, father and son, were interested in Hay Castle as a possible home for Hay's first antique shop.

The Wigingtons were from an old Stratford-upon-Avon family that had restored and sold antique furniture since Shakespeare's time. Now, however, Colin and Bryan were looking to move to Hay with their wives and Bryan's children, drawn primarily by the excellent fishing to be had in the River Wye. They looked carefully at the castle but decided, finally, on Prospect House, Broad Street. It was a 20-room house that would lend

On the right is Prospect House, where the Wigingtons opened Hay's first antique shop. On the left are Nos. 22 and 21

itself, they felt, to the needs of a three-generation family who also wanted to open a shop. And it was cheaper. So in 1964 they bought Prospect House for £4,000 and Richard Booth bought Hay Castle.

He called in to welcome them to Hay and they were grateful for the friendly gesture. 'We were incomers, and felt it', says Pat Thornton (then Pat Wigington), 'but Richard was very kind. Businesses were at that time run almost exclusively by old Hay families.'

Prospect House had been built in the classical Georgian style and the large rooms either side of the front door made an ideal setting for the Wigingtons' stock of antique furniture together with, according to Pat, 'beautiful old glass and silver of a quality now rarely seen'.

Colin Wigington is remembered today as a superb craftsman and his son, Bryan, was almost as good. He had learnt antique restoration from his father in the time-honoured tradition of passing down craftsmanship within a family. He was often referred to as Wiggy.

Wiggy's father was a brilliant man. Wiggy was good but his father was in a different league because of his wide range of skills. He built a grandfather clock from scratch, the wooden case but also the workings. He even made the metal moving parts himself. He was also a gunsmith. They were a very gifted family.

Neil Hitchcox

Pat was married to Bryan and remembers her father-in-law with affection:

He was a lovely man, very quiet and studious. He would often be in his workshop till one or two in the morning restoring and making furniture or turning the special little jeweller's lathe he had for making rings. He also restored Purdey guns, those handmade shotguns favoured by the aristocracy.

He believed that the best way to work with antique furniture was to use antique tools and many of his chisels had come down to him from his grandfather's grandfather.

In her living room in Chancery Court she had a six-drawer side table made by him in the Queen Anne style, and immaculately veneered in walnut. Also a 'pie crust' tray that he gave her for her birthday a month before he died of cancer in the early 1970s, aged just 69.

The symmetry of Prospect House suited the needs of the family in other ways too. The double extensions at the back had a courtyard garden between them, across which Pat and her mother-in-law faced each other from their own kitchens. Colin and Bryan each had their own workshop beyond that.

Though my kitchen was very primitive at the beginning. It was the one with the side entrance onto Chancery Lane and when we first arrived there was a gas cooker and a sink and not much else. The floorboards were so rotten there were holes in them and we had to stand on a board over the one in front of the sink to avoid falling through. [PT]

And the kitchen floor was not the only thing in need of repair.

> The first job we had to do when we moved in was get the wall at the front of the raised cobbles rebuilt. It was in danger of collapsing into the roadway. The cobbles in front of Prospect House were used on market days for selling eggs from. It was mostly eggs. Further up towards the clock tower it was live chickens and ducks. The children liked to go and see them. I used to buy a trayful of eggs every week from a farmer's wife from Painscastle way who used to sell mainly to people who came up from Cardiff. [PT]

That 'farmer's wife from Painscastle' had a granddaughter called Angie who now runs a café in St John's Place.

Much of Broad Street was somewhat dilapidated at that time, but the Seven Stars was falling apart. It had been de-licensed back in the 1930s and now was occupied by an old lady who was almost never seen, but lived, it was said, in just one of its many rooms. The rest lay dusty and unused. Children were told not to walk on that side of the street in windy weather in case a slate blew off the roof and hit them, as had once happened to Billie Pugh when passing the Café Royal. 'The whole building was virtually falling down. There were loads of places like that in Hay at that time.'

The Seven Stars today, after extensive renovation in the 1970s

And many would remain like that for some time to come. Certainly the Seven Stars would continue to crumble until renovated by Terry Salter in the late 1970s.

It was difficult for Pat and Bryan Wigington's five children to fit in with Hay life at first. The eldest two went to school on Oxford Road, on the site that would later house the Community Centre, while the younger ones went to the school on Heol y Dwr. As incomers, or 'blow-ins', they were obvious targets for the school bullies until they learned how to deal with them. The five-year-old came home one day with blood running down his face but saying proudly 'I won!'

The children of 1960s Hay in general, however, enjoyed much the same freedoms as those from the 1930s had done. There were still plenty of open spaces to explore and relatively few cars on the roads.

Mrs Wigington senior worked on Prospect House's garden and former orchard, which at that time passed behind the ice house to stretch halfway down Brook Street. Her greatest achievement, however, was a long herbaceous border, and she was annoyed when the family lurcher, Sam, chose it as the place in which to hide the gains from his own greatest achievement – the theft of a rack of frozen ribs of lamb from the back of a delivery van parked outside Keylock's butcher's shop on Castle Street. It was a Tuesday, early closing day, and the street was deserted. He trotted home proudly with it dangling from his jaws and headed straight for the herbaceous border to bury it. Those were the days when dogs could still roam freely and butchers would bill the owners if they caught them stealing. That rack of lamb kept Sam going for weeks.

Cars were gradually taking over, however – and, also in 1964, Hay Castle's orchard was converted into a giant car park, largely as an act of faith. At that stage it was unclear whether the town would ever attract enough visitors to justify it, and initially only a few cars would be parked there. The sloping site was seen as more useful for tobogganing down on tin trays when it snowed. Over time, however, as bookshops began to proliferate and Richard Booth's genius for self-promotion brought publicity, the visitors did come.

Underhill's Garage

It was the growing popularity of cars that, again in 1964, led Cusop farmer's daughter, Eileen Underhill, and her husband, Peter, to buy Spencer Hall's garage. It was in a dilapidated state but they were hopeful that they could make it work once some basic problems had been sorted out.

The showroom leaked badly and, when a new roof failed to solve the problem, it had to be almost completely rebuilt. But at least it was clear what needed to be done. The difficulties over the petrol pumps were more complex. In Spencer Hall's time there had been one pump and it had been on the pavement. But the petrol company were not prepared to continue that arrangement when he left. They wanted at least two pumps, and they wanted them off-street on a garage forecourt.

Underhills car showroom in its early days with the house (now demolished) where Spencer Hall had lived with his family. His petrol pump is still on the pavement.
(Photo courtesy of Ann Williams)

A painting of Underhill's Garage by Veronica Guest. (Photo courtesy of Veronica Guest)

The obvious answer was to bring the stagnant old millpond into use but Hay Urban District Council resolutely refused to sell it, perhaps because one of its most prominent councillors owned a rival garage. The problem seemed insurmountable until, finally, Peter Underhill thought of making an appeal to Hay's Member of Parliament, Tudor Watkins. He telephoned him at home and was gratified to receive a call back later that same evening. Councillors had been spoken to and the way ahead cleared.

The Underhills acquired the millpond, drained it, and sank two large petrol reservoirs, back-filling them with rubble from a derelict mill building and some hardcore left over from the creation of Hay's new car park. The pumps were then erected over the top, a small hut was provided for the petrol pump attendant and the forecourt was ready for use.

Spencer Hall had held a car franchise from Leyland, but when Peter Underhill applied to take it over he was told at the interview to go back and first prove that he could make it work. Spencer Hall had struggled to sell enough cars; could he do better? He could. He and Eileen managed to make £1,000 profit in their first year. Leyland granted him the franchise, and Underhills Garage went from strength to strength.

The lower part of the Underhill's site, previously used to park buses, was now occupied by post office vans. Postman Raymond Pugh and his friend, Reuben Watkins, made sure that the post was delivered in even the most difficult of weathers, and that the occupants of isolated farmsteads were not left neglected. When snow prevented the vans being taken out they would use bicycles, pushing them over fields if necessary, especially if they knew it was a child's birthday. Many a time they would be asked if they could 'pop in and have a look at my iron that's on the blink', or something similar, and they were happy to oblige.

Close-up of the bicycle wheel, with the legend 'Rest for the Tyred'

Today, Postman Pugh's daughters run Londis Pugh, the grocer's on High Town, where they continue their father's tradition of cheerful willingness to go the extra mile. This was especially appreciated during the Covid lockdown of 2020/21 when entry to shops was forbidden and those who were unable to queue in the cold outside had to rely on home deliveries. Reuben Watkin's daughter works with them, along with their other dedicated staff.

Underhills Garage would be a major feature of Broad Street for 40 years, only closing when Peter and Eileen retired in 2005. Today the site is occupied by the Millbank housing estate.

The Seventies

In 1975 Broad Street lost two of its most popular and long-standing shops at virtually the same time. Nellie Lewis's butcher's shop had been so well patronised that the queue had stretched right up the road on a Saturday morning. But now she sold it and the slaughterhouse to Ellis Morgan. And on the other side of the entryway Eric and Neil Hitchcox closed the doors of the Café Royal for the last time.

In 1973 Eric Hitchcox sold all three of his premises, the Black Swan, the Café Royal and the Tea Room at auction as one lot

Back in the 1920s a bent bicycle wheel had been mounted above the door with the legend 'Rest for the Tyred'. The wheel had come from a postman's bicycle, left at the kerbside and run over by a cart. The words aimed to encourage members of the cycling clubs that proliferated after the First World War to stop there for refreshment. Now, however, they were more applicable to the proprietor himself. Eric Hitchcox was indeed tired and in need of rest.

He had closed the bakery when Dai Ratcliffe had left to work for himself some time before. The building had needed complete refurbishment with new ovens, and he refused to spend money on such things. All the bread he sold from then on was Mother's Pride.

Back in 1970 he had been knocked for six when his eldest son Graham, who had run the Café Royal with him, died of Hodgkinson's Lymphoma. Neil was called back from Australia, where he had emigrated as a 'ten pound Pom', and the service then offered by him and his father would be long-remembered.

> Remember when Mr Hitchcox and his son Neil ran the grocery shop here? We shall never see again the sort of service they gave – not in supermarkets that's for certain.
>
> HAYWIRE 87

But Eric's appetite for work was waning and in 1973 he made a serious attempt to retire. All three of his premises, the Tea Room, the Café Royal and the Black Swan, were put up for auction as one lot. Messrs Russell, Baldwin and Bright (now Chancellors) of Church Street conducted the sale, which was held at the Crown – and to everyone's surprise, including her husband's, they were bought by Anna Golesworthy.

Anna's husband, Roger, had other ideas, however, and the whole complex was soon back on the market, though it proved more difficult to sell the second time around. The buildings were run down, and mortgage rates were as high as 15%. Geoff and Amy Price were still tenants of the Black Swan, and so for two years Eric and Neil continued to run the Café Royal under Golesworthy ownership to help make it more attractive to potential buyers. But it was all to no avail. In 1975 Eric finally gave up, closing the doors for the last time on the Café Royal his mother had opened 74 years earlier.

It would remain empty until John Thomas – known as John the Fish from his fish shop on Lion Street, where Potty Watkin's bakery had been – bought the whole complex in 1979. He retained the name of the Café Royal but reopened it as a steak bar after extensive refurbishment. The old post office building became a fish and chip shop that would, some time later, be run by Dai Ratcliffe, the former baker. It is now Hay Takeaway.

Richard Booth creates a Booktown

By 1975 it was apparent that the heart was going out of small towns and villages all over the country, as supermarkets and chain stores took the trade from local shops. In Hay the mushrooming of grocers that had followed the opening of the railway was now in reverse. They, and other shops, were closing and remaining empty. By 1976 general unemployment in Wales had reached a level where the Westminster Government felt obliged to step in, and the Welsh Development Agency was created in an attempt to address the problem. A year later it was joined by the Development Board for Rural Wales, usually known as the DBRW.

But government agencies were anathema to Richard Booth. He disliked bureaucracy and all that it stood for. Hay would, he felt, be able to sustain itself perfectly well without government intervention if it could be reinvented as a 'booktown'.

Frank English was noted both for his prodigious alcohol consumption and for the miles of wooden shelving (some said even hundreds of miles) he built for Richard Booth at the Cinema Bookshop, the Castle and The Limited

 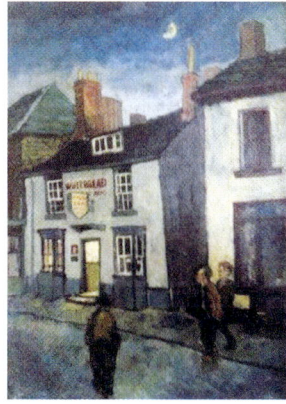

LEFT: Richard Booth as a young man, with Vi Jenkins, landlady of the Mason's Arms.

RIGHT: A painting of the Masons Arms on Castle Street, now the SPAR. (Photo courtesy of Kelvyn Jenkins)

Opinions differ as to who it was that first came up with the then completely novel idea of promoting Hay as a booktown. But Kelvyn Jenkins, who grew up in the Mason's Arms, believes it originated one convivial night in the bar there with bookshelf-builder extraordinaire, Frankie English.

If the idea had been put forward at a meeting of the DBRW it would no doubt have been dismissed as laughable. How was it possible to hope that 20 or so closed shops could reopen and make a profit by selling only second-hand books in a small town where reading had never been a top priority? But Richard was not proceeding by means of meetings. He was already bringing vast quantities of books into the town and opening outlets for them. All that was needed now, he believed, was lots of publicity.

Richard Booth, the self-styled King of Hay, in front of his castle.
(Photo courtesy of Hereford Libraries)

So, he gave full rein to his love of a joke and came up with an idea for a stunt that would simultaneously gain publicity for Hay as a booktown, and satisfy his need to be a big fish in a small pond. On April Fools' Day 1977, with a burnished gas pipe for a sceptre in one hand and a lavatory ballcock for an orb in the other, he had himself declared King of the Independent Kingdom of Hay.

And it worked. The media loved the eccentricity of it all and Hay was suddenly in the public eye once more. It had not received so much attention since the Armstrong affair 55 years earlier. Book-lovers flocked in, and with them came creatives and free-thinkers, all eager to join the fun at the court of King Richard – and perhaps make a living at the same time.

Though it was local people who did the bulk of the work, as Richard both acknowledged and encouraged. For the great quantities of books he was bringing into the town required a small army of loaders, lorry and van drivers; shop fitters and shelf stackers; researchers, cataloguers and salespeople; buyers and people to go with him on his extended buying trips. Not that these roles were necessarily kept distinct.

Extrovert and expansive, Richard's first drinking-place of choice had been the snug of the Crown Hotel, patronised by the local gentry. He was, after all, from the Booths of Brynmelyn. Their money had come from Booth's Gin, while his mother had been a Yardley heiress. But the Crown was not really his kind of place and he soon migrated to the Masons Arms on Castle Street (now SPAR) where there was more fun to be had. Here, he could carouse with the manual workers and lorry drivers who, he often said, formed 'the backbone of the rural economy' – a phrase that was never very far from his lips.

> Pride in manual work, I believe, is the basis of any traditional rural economy. I hold a good manual worker in higher esteem than any intellectual. Working with just a few country labourers, I ended up possessing books of greater intellectual variety than all the universities in the British Isles put together.[3]

Richard generally felt uneasy around university graduates. He himself had been to Oxford but left prematurely. Underneath the shambling, shirt-hanging-out persona with which he fronted the booktown enterprise, however, was an instinctive knowledge of how to choose good staff, and this did occasionally lead him to employ one. Conversations something like the following might take place from time to time:

> I'm looking for a job, Richard. Have you got anything I could do?
> Um, er, er, are you a graduate?
> Yes
> Hmm. Er, um, well. You see bookselling is, er, is a manual job. There is, er, there's a lot of lifting and carrying involved.

Then would come his great guffaw of a laugh as an idea came to him:

> Perhaps you could open a cookery bookshop for me. I've got a container-full of American cookery books coming in from the States and nowhere to put them.

The number of bookshops rose steadily. Geoffrey Aspin, formerly a lecturer in the north of England, moved to Hay and put his stock of French literature into what had been Keylock's butcher's shop on Castle Street. Derek Addyman and several others left Richard's employ to open shops of their own, and by the 1990s there were somewhere between 30 and 40 bookshops in Hay, along with associated bookbinders and print shops.

The largest premises were owned by Richard himself. Using inherited money, he had bought Frank Lewis House, once owned by James Spencer but sold, as Spencer's fortunes declined, to become the workhouse. Hay's once-popular cinema, now made redundant by television, became the Hay Cinema Bookshop, as it still is today, though now run by a co-operative of former employees. And the old Agricultural Hall on Lion Street, usually known as 'The Limited',[4] was also shelved out from top to bottom for the sale of books.

But the largest building of all, Hay castle, became both antiquarian bookshop and royal residence. The King was in his castle.

Hay Library

Back in 1947, Betty Breeze had been 17 and working at Hay Urban District Council's offices in Belle Vue at the top of Broad Street. Young and enthusiastic, she had readily agreed to the suggestion that she might like to start a library for the town, and was only mildly daunted by the discovery that it was to consist solely of two boxes of books and a cupboard. She made the best of it, however, and for one hour per week, on a Monday, loaned out books kept in the old Methodist chapel on Oxford Road. It was enough to start her on a long career. She would remain Hay's librarian for the next 45 years.

That one hour a week was soon extended to two, one on Monday and one on Friday, and as the stock of books expanded, the premises changed to a small shop on High Town (now the chandelier shop next to Oxfam). The next move took it into the council offices themselves (in the former vicarage, Belle Vue) as part of a cost-cutting exercise, but this proved highly unsatisfactory. There were always boxes of books all over the floor. It was clearly time for Hay's library to have a dedicated site of its own.

The lodging houses and lines of small cottages along Chancery Lane had been demolished a few years earlier in what many had thought an unnecessary clearance. Pat Wigington, whose garden was alongside, was one of those who felt that they had been of historic interest and should have been upgraded and retained. By 1974 they were gone, however, and the space they had occupied was available.

Local government reforms of that year meant that most of the powers formerly held by Hay Urban District Council were transferred to Brecon, leaving Hay with a relatively powerless community council. So it was Brecknock Borough Council that, in 1975, erected a purpose-built library in Chancery Lane. The council wanted to obtain clearer access to the library by putting a compulsory purchase order on the garage attached to Prospect House and demolishing it. That idea was dropped, however, when it was found that the space alongside the garage was already wider than the entrance in from Broad Street. Betty Jones, née Breeze, was delighted with the new library. 'It was a real treat to have proper shelves for the books'.

1978–1981

Jo Leighton was born at 11 o'clock one Thursday market day morning in 1967, in the house that would later become the Granary bar. She was Arthur Golesworthy's first great-grandchild and a large congratulatory fish was presented to him by the fish stall. Other stallholders came too, with gifts from the stalls that were all up and down Broad Street at that time. Everyone knew everyone else and the news had travelled fast.

Broad Street was full of children in those days, in sharp contrast to today when there are none. They played outdoors in each other's often large gardens and the wooded riverbanks either side of the Wye. Nobody thought then that children should only go out under adult supervision. They would roam through the town, sometimes coming across Richard Booth on his way to one or other of his various premises, and were gratified when he remembered their names.

Jo was 11 years old when her close friends, the Wigington children, left Broad Street. Mrs Wigington senior had been widowed and was anxious to return to her family in Stratford-upon-Avon so, in 1978, Prospect House was sold. Pat and Bryan Wigington split up after 29 years of marriage and Pat arranged for Bryan's workshop to be moved to the basement of

Pat Thornton on her 80th birthday

the disused chapel that is now The Globe. He would reopen Wigington Antiques in No. 14 Broad Street before later moving to nearby Eardisley. Pat would re-marry and become Pat Thornton.

Pat had taken a part-time job with Richard Booth back in 1974, working at Brynmelyn on Cusop Dingle in a large shed that was so cold she hardly took her coat off for two years. Her job was to catalogue the long runs of periodicals, mostly from America, that were stacked high on metal shelving. Universities bought great quantities from her catalogues, until their grants were halved. But the trade in periodicals went on diminishing year on year, even after that, as first microfiche and then computers took over.

It was a relief to Pat then, when she moved down to work first at the Castle and then The Limited,[4] taking charge of the theology and philosophy sections. It was a job she loved and would continue in until her mid-80s.

Two years after the Wigington's house was sold, the Webbs went too. There had been a Webb presence on the street for 60 years. Humphrey Webb retired in 1979, the year that John Thomas bought the Café Royal. He closed down the undertaking business and sold the garage where the hearse had been kept to Alan Powell. It became a carpentry workshop, complete with the planing machine that had once been used for the coffins in the Webb's garage on Lion Street, and remains so today albeit under new ownership.

When Humphrey died later that same year the rest of the Webb complex on Broad Street was split up and sold, the conveyance dated 30 September 1980.

The first of Broad Street's bookshops had opened in 1979 and, somewhat surprisingly, it dealt solely with poetry. The poet Anne Stevenson (perhaps best-known today for her controversial but brilliant biography of Sylvia Plath, *Bitter Fame*) was living in Hay at the end of the 1970s. 'The Poetry Bookshop', she would later write, 'was a mad-cap idea of the 1970s. Michael Farley and I, in rebellion against Oxford academics, bourgeois gentility and the very concept of money as a way of life (Capitalism), escaped to Hay in the summer of 1978.'[5]

She and Michael Farley first set up shop in the former workhouse at the far end of town, but then moved to No. 22 Broad Street. They had no money with which to start a business; so, ingeniously, they stocked the shelves with spare poetry books of their own and supplemented these with duplicate stock begged from a dealer in Oxford. And, somewhat to their own surprise, it worked. They would leave town in 1981 but the shop continued. Today, the Poetry Bookshop is run by Chris and Melanie, and operates from large premises at the bottom of the Pavement.

Broad Street's next second-hand bookshop would be another specialist one, this time selling only children's books. It would be run by Ron and Sheila Rose from No. 14, the front wall of which was painted pink to go with the name 'Rose's Bookshop'. Ownership would change in time but the pink wall would remain a feature of that end of the street until 2021 when it was dramatically repainted in dark grey. Other houses up and down the street would become bookshops over the years, but today the only one remaining is the Broad Street Book Centre at No. 6, the former home of the Café Royal.

The demise of Eric Hitchcox's café had left a gap in the market, and in 1979 the four adult children of Roger and Anna Golesworthy decided to try their hand at running a teashop in the family-owned granary on Broad Street. Their great-grandfather, F.W. Golesworthy, had acquired the building at the end of the previous century and over the years it had been a school and an auction house before being rented out to a farmers' co-operative. Their

The Granary

childhood memories were of huge bales of wool being hoisted up to the first floor and stored there before being lowered back to the ground floor and sold. Caroline had done a course at catering college in Hereford and specialised in cake-making. She and Jeannette would do the catering between them with the books of cookery writer, Elizabeth David, as their bibles. They began with just tea, cakes and scones, employing Jo, aged 13, as the waitress when she wasn't at school. Within a couple of years, however, they were well on their way to earning a place in *Just a Bite*, Egon Ronay's prestigious café directory. The Granary would remain popular for the next 40 years and is still flourishing today.

AFTERWORD

By 1981 the sense of community that had once been such a feature of life on Broad Street was slipping away, with more cars on the road and fewer children. Most of the market stalls would move to Memorial Square in front of the castle during the 1980s and the street would become more of a backwater.

The Crown Hotel, once such a focus of social life, would be converted to flats, and a large shop selling teddy bears and jigsaws, by a new resident called Leon K. Morelli. He would change the name of Prospect House to Chancery House and block the Right of Way across his section of the raised cobbled pavement by erecting railings round it. Old Mr Mayall, watchmaker of High Town, would come down and shake his stick at them. A large part of the garden at the back, once Mrs Wigington senior's pride and joy, was sold off for housing and is now Kemys Place, Brook Street.

Both Leon Morelli and, from 1988 onwards, the *Hay Festival of Literature* would challenge Richard Booth's pre-eminent position in the town. But the notion of Hay as a Town of Books had taken hold and would remain. Today there are booktowns worldwide, much as Richard had prophesied and worked to promote. He died in August 2019 and is buried in Cusop churchyard.

The Three Tuns, to which Leslie Powell had moved his family in 1922, is now a restaurant. Lucy died in March 2017 but her memory lives on. Before he too died, aged 97, her younger brother Albert thought back over her life:

There was that big fire [in 2005]. Lucy came to live with me for six months after that. It was the first time she had ever lived anywhere except the Three Tuns. She would never go to bed before two or three in the morning. I would say 'Lucy GO TO BED!' Then she'd be tired in the day. One day when she'd fallen asleep by the fire in the Three Tuns someone came in and took the till, money and all. It was one of those old-fashioned wooden tills. They just lifted the whole thing while she was sleeping by the fire.

Lucy and her brother, Albert, in the Three Tuns. (Photo courtesy of Diane Nicholls)

Perhaps in some alternative universe Lucy still sleeps by a coal fire in a small grate and dreams of dancing in the Parish Hall, or swimming in the Wye. Of the celebrations when the tolls came off the bridge in 1933; or of Mr Wilson, the dentist, drinking in her bar one afternoon and forgetting about little Tony Pugh, left screaming in his surgery across the road. Or perhaps of black American soldiers assembling in the back bar of the Three Tuns during the Second World War and singing their harmonious spirituals.

ENDNOTES

Chapter 1

1. ... and apparently never had been. There have been several small archaeological excavations in various parts of the town over the years but nothing has been found that dates from before the medieval period. A Roman coin was picked up in the garden of 6 Broad Street by Jennifer Hitchcox when she was a child and her father sent it to Cardiff. He got a letter back begging to acknowledge the receipt of:

    A copper coin (3AE) of Constantine the Great (306–337 AD)
    'Gloria Exercitus' type, Constantinople mint

    for inclusion in the collections of the National Museum of Wales. But finding a Roman coin in Hay was a rare, not to say unique, event. Writing in 1808 Theophilus Jones noted that 'no Roman coins have been found here within the memory of man'. *(Glanusk Edn,* p. 99) It has sometimes been said that there was no Roman road on the Hay side of the Wye but there is some evidence to the contrary and the matter deserves further consideration. There were two, possibly three, Roman camps within the great loop of the Wye east of Hay. (Keith Ray, Ch. 5)

2. The border between England and Wales varied over the years but seems to have run along the course of the Dulais in the early Norman period, as it does today. Keith Ray notes that, 'By the 11th century, English settlement had extended along the south bank [of the Wye] to Clifford and Cusop right up to the present-day border by Hay-on-Wye.' (p. 218) There is also the fact that Hay is not mentioned in Domesday Book, which recorded English lands, whereas Cusop is.

3. The motte by the Wye at Clifford would not be surmounted by the large structure in stone whose ruins can be seen today until sometime after 1075.

4. A haye was thus a kind of, usually small, deer park though they could be quite large. A number of Anglo-Saxon haga (hayes) that were in existence before the Conquest are now documented as deer parks.

5   Frank and Caroline Thorn (eds) *Domesday Book, Vol 17 Herefordshire*, p. 340.

6   J.E. Lloyd, 'Wales and the Coming of the Normans 1039–1093' in Transactions of the Honourable Society of Cymmrodorion, 1901, p. 162.

7   Hay Castle Trust website (Dec 2020) gives that somewhere towards the end of the 11th century or the beginning of the 12th the top of the hill at Hay was circled by an earthen ringwork with a stone gate-tower.

8   C.G Portman, *The Sacred Stones, Sacred Trees, and Holy Wells of Hay* has much to say about the mythology attached to these wells.

9   Gerald of Wales, *The Journey Through Wales*.

10 'Anne Mortimer was the grandmother of Yorkist King Edward IV and Richard III. By way of Edward's daughter, Elizabeth of York, every monarch of England and, subsequently, the United Kingdom, from Henry VIII up to and including Elizabeth II, is descended in a direct line from Sybil de Neufmarché.' Alan Nicholls, *The Lords of Hay*, p. 18 (Anne Mortimer was descended from Edward III's son, Lionel, duke of Clarence).

11 ibid p. 23.

12 R.W. Banks, *The Early History of Hay and its Lordship*, p. 177.

13 Evidence that Hay's charter did indeed confer these special privileges on its burgage holders comes from a document of 1340 (see Chapter 9). This gives the annual burgage charge (as distinct from the rent) as a mere 12d a year and makes it clear that many burgages were being sublet. According to Fairs, these were signs that the Laws of Breteuil were in operation.

14 William Rees, *An Historical Atlas of Wales*.

15 The name has various forms including de Breos and de Briose.

16 Gerald of Wales, *The Journey Through Wales*.

17 A conclusion drawn from toll receipts by both William Rees and Geoffrey Fairs (p. 49).

18 From *Brut y Tywysogian* quoted by Alan Nicholls in *The Lords of Hay*, p. 49.

CHAPTER 2

1   R.W. Banks, *The Early History of Hay and its Lordship*, p. 181.

2   From *Annales Camb.* quoted by Nicholls in *The Lords of Hay*, p.55.

3   From *Close Rolls* quoted by Nicholls in *The Lords of Hay*, p. 56.

4   R.W. Banks, *The Early History of Hay and its Lordship*, p. 182.

5 Some of the houses along Oxford Road today back onto the lower part of the town wall, which rises high from the level of Oxford Road to form the end of the Bear Street burgage plots. Thus on all three sides of the town there was a steep drop on the outer side of the wall, giving defenders the advantage of height.

6 R.W. Banks, *The Early History of Hay and its Lordship*, p. 182.

7 *The Survey of Acreage and Rental of Welsh Hay and English Hay* (trans. Richard Morgan in *Brycheiniog* Vol. 28 1995–96).

8 Geoffrey Fairs, *A History of The Hay*, p. 42 and endnote 6.

9 R.W. Banks, *The Early History of Hay and its Lordship*, p. 185.

10 Alan Nicholls, *Historical Directory of Hay on Wye*, p. 578 gives that in 1902 there was a proposal to widen Heol y Dwr by removing the old Tuck Mill, setting back the wall of the garden of Poplar House, and putting the mill stream into pipes.

11 Kate Clarke, *The Book of Hay*, p. 14.

12 William Gilpin, *Observations on the River Wye*, for example, though it was a widely held assumption, also held by John Leland.

13 Quoted by Hay Millennium Society, *Nobody Had Heard of Hay*, p. 8.

14 Quoted by David Ross, *Wales: History of a Nation*, p. 123.

15 Leland's *Itinerary*, Vol 3, p. 110.

16 Geoffrey Fairs, *A History of the Hay*, p. 49.

17 B.G. Charles, *Non-Celtic Place-Names in Wales*.

18 Leland's *Itinerary*, Vol 4, p. 166.

19 Geoffrey Fairs, *A History of the Hay*, p. 29.

20 'Mr Gwyn and his brother-in-law ... are stated ... to have imprisoned several persons and to have extorted large sums by way of toll from those who came here to fairs and markets, but upon their appearance and disclaimer ... the trifling crimes of false imprisonment and extortion [were] forgotten or forgiven.' (Theophilus Jones, *History of the County of Brecknock*, Glanusk edn, p. 100).

CHAPTER 3

1 Jones & Smith, 'Houses of Breconshire' in *Brycheiniog*, Vol 10, p. 154.

2 Geoffrey Fairs, *A History of the Hay*, p. 241.

3 CADW *Buildings of Special Architectural or Historic Interest: Hay on Wye*.

4 See Dineley's drawing of the castle in Chapter 13.

5   Geoffrey Fairs, *A History of the Hay*, p. 209.

6   Theophilus Jones, *History of the County of Brecknock*, p. 100.

7   These were reconstituted forms of the position held a century before by the fearsome bishop, Rowland Lee. The Council had been revived by Edward IV and was based at Ludlow.

8   Under the grand title: *The Account of the Official Progress of His Grace, Henry, the First Duke of Beaufort through Wales in 1684*. The part that relates to Hay is quoted in Fairs, *A History of the Hay*, p. 51.

9   Belmont Road was originally a section of the main road through town which had continued past the church and on to Glasbury and Brecon. Since Castle Street had been built, however, it had become something of a back street. At some later point it would also be known as Tabernacle Row, after the Nonconformist chapel that once occupied the site now taken by the Catholic Church.

10 Leland's *Itinerary* Vol 2, p. 69.

11 A pound was a holding yard for stray animals. Poplar House, which stands there today, was formerly called Pound Head.

12 Fairs, *A History of the Hay*, p. 250.

13 *ibid* p. 82.

14 *ibid* plate 26.

CHAPTER 4

1   Fairs *Annals of a Parish*, Ch. 13.

2   The full text of this Act, written by Spencer, is bound into the company's Minutes Book (HARC N44/1).

3   C.R. Clinker, *The Hay Railway*.

4   Rattenbury and Cook, *The Hay and Kington Railways*, p. 25.

5   The River Wye makes a dramatic double loop just before it passes Hay and inside the first of these is a large grassy area called The Warren. The Normans reintroduced rabbits to Britain (there had been a few in Roman times) and created artificial warrens to provide 'living larders' of rabbit meat. It is likely, then, that the Hay warren was established in Norman times. Rabbit skins and fur were widely used for clothing.

6   Geoffrey Fairs, *A History of the Hay*, p. 268.

7   William H. Smith, *The Hereford, Hay and Brecon Branch*, p. 86.

8   David Bennett, *A Local History of the Pubs and Inns of Hay-on-Wye*, p. 71.

9   David Bennett, A *Local History of the Rose and Crown*, p. 15.

10 David Bennett, *A Local History of the Pubs and Inns of Hay-on-Wye*, p. 7.

11 Fairs, *A History of the Hay*, p. 155.

12 Robin Saikia, *Blue Guide to Hay-on-Wye*, p. 65.

13 Richard Haslam, *Powys: The Buildings of Wales* series, Yale.

14 Eisel and Bennett, *The Pubs of Hay-on-Wye and the Golden Valley*.

15 John Godfrey William's Notes, pp. 11/12 gives:

   Lease for 14 years dated 20 Aug 1872 Sir Joseph Russell Bailey Bart to Wm Terrett of the Old Mill situate in Water St, formerly occupied by Robert Williams at £6 p.a. Formerly this old mill leased by John Pratt etc c. 1860

16 Fairs, *A History of the Hay*, p. 107.

17 ibid p. 109.

18 In Kilvert's time the post office was in Radnor House, on the corner of Oxford Road and Church Street.

Chapter 5

1   Eric Pugh, *My Father's Life in Hay*.

2   Cutting taken from an unidentified local newspaper.

3   Fairs, *A History of the Hay*, p. 119.

4   ibid p. 109.

5   Alan Nicholls, *Hay at War 1914–1918*, p. 11.

6   ibid p. 17.

7   ibid p. 11.

8   ibid p. 95.

9   ibid p. 113.

Chapter 6

1   Robin Odell, *Exhumation of a Murder*, p. 55.

2   ibid.

3   Martin Beales, *The Hay Poisoner*.

4   Odell, *Exhumation of a Murder*, p. 197.

5 Beales, *The Hay Poisoner*, p. 225.

6 David Bennett, *Major Injustice*, Ch. 10.

CHAPTER 7

1 Unpublished paper by Des Madigan, who ran Hay's cinema for many years.

2 Eisel and Bennett, *Pubs of Hay-on-Wye and the Golden Valley*, p. 204.

3 Landowning women had had the vote until 1832, but lost it in the Great Reform Bill of that year which specified that only men could vote. The franchise would be extended to all women in 1928.

4 Hay Millennium Soc., *Nobody Had Heard of Hay*, p. 30, reprinted from *The Wye* magazine.

5 Hundreds of similar small companies were formed throughout England and Wales during the nineteenth century, though they were all nationalised in May 1949 when the industry was reshaped under twelve regional Gas Boards. The Gas Act of 1972 then brought all the boards together to form the British Gas Corporation, commonly known as British Gas.

6 Fairs, *A History of the Hay*, p. 118.

7 Cats' Park was the name given to a pull-in area, with trees between it and the road. Used by lorry drivers taking a break and said to have been frequented by working girls. The land had previously been occupied by a line of cottages known as Chain Alley, described by Theophilus Jones (p. 102) as 'A line of thirteen cottages and a refreshment house, the whole presenting a most disreputable appearance'. They were demolished in 1870.

8 Robert Golesworthy, *Roger's War*.

9 ibid.

CHAPTER 9

1 Geoffrey Fairs, *Annals of a Parish*, p. 26.

2 They were coming, in the main, from country house libraries whose English and Irish owners had fallen on hard times in the changing social climate of post-war Britain. But container-loads were also being sent back from America.

3 Richard Booth, *My Kingdom of Books*, p. 21.

4 The agricultural hall had been a large shop selling farm equipment and machinery, run by Robert Williams. His company became the first limited company in Hay and this building has generally been known as 'The Limited' ever since.

5 From a letter to Chris and Melanie of the present Poetry Bookshop.

BIBLIOGRAPHY

Banks, R.W., 'The Early History of Hay and its Lordship' in *Archaeologia Cambrensis,* Vol. 14 (1883)
Beales, Martin, *Dead Not Buried*, Robert Hale, 1995
 (reprinted as *The Hay Poisoner: The Trial of Major Herbert Rowse Armstrong* by PMB Press, 2013)
Bennett, David, *Local History of the Rose and Crown*, s.p., 2014
— *A Local History of the Pubs and Inns of Hay-on-Wye*, s.p., 2015
— *Major Injustice: The Case of Herbert Rowse Armstrong*, s.p., 2015
Booth, Richard, *My Kingdom of Books*, s.p., 1999
Brecknock Soc. (pub), *Brycheiniog*, Vols 10, 16 and 28
Charles, B.G., *Non-Celtic Place-Names in Wales,* University College London, 1938
Clarke, Kate, *The Book of Hay*, Logaston Press, 2015
CADW *Buildings of Special Architectural or Historic Interest: Hay on Wye,* Listed buildings as at 1 Feb 1988
Clinker, C.R., *The Hay Railway*, David Charles, 1960
Crow, Alan, *Bridges on the River Wye*, Lapridge Publications, 1995
Davies, Dewi, *Brecknock Historian*, Evans, 1977
Davies, Lewis, *Radnorshire*, Cambridge University Press, 1912
Eisel, John and Bennett, Frank, *The Pubs of Hay-on-Wye and the Golden Valley*, Logaston Press, 2005
Erskine, Barbara, *The Lady of Hay*, Michael Joseph, 1986
Evans, Christopher, *Breconshire*, Cambridge University Press, 1912
Fairs, Geoffrey L., *A History of the Hay: The Story of Hay-on-Wye*, Phillimore, 1972
— *Annals of a Parish: A Short History of Hay-on-Wye*, s.p., 1994
Ford, Dr Peter, *Matilda, Lady of Hay*, Logaston Press, 2021
Gerald of Wales, *The Journey Through Wales* (Trans. Lewis Thorpe), Penguin Classics, 1978
Gilpin, William, *Observations on the River Wye*, printed for R. Blamire, 1782; reprinted by Pallas Athene, 2005
Golesworthy, Robert, *Roger's War*, unpublished

Gregory, Donald, *Radnorshire: A Historical Guide*, Gwasg Carreg Gwalch, 1994
Haslam, Richard, *Powys: The Buildings of Wales Series* (ed. Pevsner), University of Wales Press/ Penguin, 1979
Hay History Group, *Hay on Wye History Notes 2018*
Hay Millennium Society, *Nobody Had Heard of Hay*, Logaston Press, 2002
Hitchcox, Neil, *My Life in Hay*, unpublished paper
Howse, W.H., *Radnorshire*, Thurston, 1949
Hume, Philip, *The Welsh Marcher Lordships 1: Central and North*, Logaston Press, 2021
Jones and Smith, 'Houses of Breconshire' in *Brycheiniog* Vol 10
Jones, Theophilus, *History of the County of Brecknock,* W. and G. North, 1809; Glanusk edition, 1909
Leland, John *(see Smith, Lucy)*
Le Quesne, A.L., *After Kilvert*, OUP, 1978
Levine, Norma, *Chronicles of Love and Death*, Vajra Publications (n.d.)
Lloyd, Prof. J.E., 'Wales and the Coming of the Normans 1039–1093' in *Transactions of the Honourable Society of Cymmrodorion*, 1901
Moule, R. (ed.), *Haywire* (local news sheet), Editions 1–90, 1985–2002
Madigan, Desmond, *Entertainment in Hay*, unpublished paper
Nicholls, Alan, *Hay at War 1914–1918*, self-published, 2015
—*Historical Directory of Hay on Wye*, 2nd edition, 2015
—*Historical Directory of Hay on Wye: Rural Parish*, self-published, 2016
—*The Lords of Hay*, self published, 2016
Nelson, L.H., *The Normans in South Wales 1070–1171*, 1966
Odell, Robin, *Exhumation of a Murder: The Life and Trial of Major Armstrong*, Souvenir Press, 1975; reprinted 1988
Plomer, William (ed.), *Selections from the Diary of the Rev. Francis Kilvert*, Jonathan Cape, 1938; reprinted 2006 by O'Donoghue, Hay-on-Wye
Portman C.G., *The Sacred Stones, Sacred Trees, and Holy Wells of Hay and the Neighbourhood*, H.R. Grant, Hay, 1907
Pugh, Eric, *Old Hay in Pictures and Prints*, POH publications, 2002
— *My Father's Life in Hay*, unpublished, 2012
— *The Town of Hay, Then and Now*, self-published, 2013
Rattenbury, Gordon and Cook, Ray, *The Hay and Kington Railways*, Railway and Canal Historical Society, 1996
Ray, Keith, *The Archaeology of Herefordshire*, Logaston Press, 2015
Rees, William, 'The Medieval Lordship of Brecon', in *Transactions of the Honourable Society of Cymmrodorion*, 1915–16 (reprinted 1968 by the Brecknock Society)
—*An Historical Atlas of Wales from early to modern times*, 1951, 2nd edition
Remfry, Paul, *Hay on Wye Castle, 1066 to 1298*, SCS Publications, 1995
Ross, David, *Wales: History of a Nation*, Waverley, new edition 2010
Saikia, Robin, *Blue Guide to Hay-on-Wye*, Somerset Books, 2010
Smith, Lucy Toulmin (ed.), *The Itinerary of John Leland*, Southern Illinois University Press, 1964

Smith, Wayne, *The Drovers' Roads of the Middle Marches*, Logaston Press, 2013
Smith, William H., *The Hereford, Hay and Brecon Branch*, KRM, 2008
Stapleton, E.J., 'An Evacuee in the Hay', self-published, 2012
Thorn, Frank and Caroline (eds.), *Domesday Book, Vol 17, Herefordshire,* Phillimore, 1983
Williams, John Godfrey, Handwritten notes on foolscap paper from his years as a solicitor in the offices that are now Williams Beales. Unpublished.
Young, Filson (ed.), 'Trial of Herbert Rowse Armstrong', in *Notable British Trials Series*, William Hodge, *c.*1927

INDEX

Abergavenny 17–8
Acton, William 53
Addyman, Derek 174
Agnest (or Nest de Neufmarché) 10–11
Armstrong, Herbert Rowse viii, 58, *76*, 78, 82, 98, 105–18, *107*, *114*, 121, 151, 172
Armstrong, Katharine 107, 113–6, 120–1, 126, 128

Bailiff 9, 38
Baptists 72–3, 105
Barber, George 119, *120*, 121
Beales, Martin vii, 112, 115
Bennett, David 74, 76, 115
Bevan, Revd W.L. (later Archdeacon) 72, 81, 89, 91
Birch, Mr 129, 157
Black Mountains *x*, 1, 9, 25, 42, 138, 141
Booth, Richard 33, 51, 104, 161–2, 165, 170–4, *171*, *172*, 176, 179
Boyle, James 38, 40
de Braose family 16–7
  Eva (née Marshal) 24–5
  Giles (d.1215) 22
  Matilda (de St Valery, d.1210) 17–9, *20*, *21*, 25
  Reginald (d.*c*.1228) 22, 24
  William (d.1190) 16
  William (d.1211) 17–8, 22
  William (d.1210) 22
  William V (d.1230) 24
Brecon *x*, 9–10, 16, *19*, 24, 32, 58, 60, 92–3, 101, 105, 133, 156, 159, 175
  Battle of 5
  High Sheriff of 43
  lordship of *x*, 5, 14, 31
Brecon and Abergavenny Canal 58, 60
Brecon County Times 101, 104, 117
Breconshire 31, 41, 59
Bredwardine 73, 112
Breeze family 135
  Bert 136, 138
  Betty (later Jones) 132–3, 135, *135*, 174–5
  Bob 132
  Ivor 132
  June 133, *135*
Breteuil, Normandy 4, 16
Breteuil, Laws of 16, 27
de Breteuil, Roger (son of William FitzOsbern) 4
brooks and rivers
  Dulais Brook 1–4, 6, *19*, 43, 61–3, 70, 119
  Login Brook 3–4, 7–8, *8*, *19*, *61*
  River Wye *vi*, 1, *8*, 11, *13*, 17, *19*, 32, *42*, 47, *61*, *90*, 161
Brycheiniog *x*, 1–5, 9, *19*
Brynmelyn *see Cusop Dingle*
Buckingham, dukes of 37
Builth *x*, 1, 16–7, 36, 47
buses 70, 146, 155–6, 167

Cadman, Frank (miller and seedsmerchant) 85, 129–30, *129*
carpentry workshop 120, 176–7
cars 98, 119, 121, 128, 156, 165–7, 179
castles 2, 5, 24, 28
cattle 9, 14, 29, 43, 47–8, 50, 71, *84*, *152*
Cheese, Arthur 75–8
Cheese, Edmund Hall 75–8, 98
Chepstow 2, 23
Christianity 7–8
Clifford 2–3, 6, 11, 26, 43, 50, 148
Clyro *x*, 32, 48, 71, *90*, 133, 161
coal 58–9, 61, 62–3, 66, 122, 136–7, 159
Coles, Mr (baker and healer) 148–50
Cromwell, Thomas 31–3, 37
Cusop 114, 157, 166, 179
Cusop Dingle *x*, 114–5
  Brynmelyn 161, 173, 176

dancing 117–8, 122, 143–4
Davies, Fred (chemist) *81*, 108–10, *109*, 113–4
Davies, Tom (grocer) 85
deer 3
Dineley, Thomas 42–7, *44*, *46*, 51, 73
Domesday Book 4, 16

Elfael *x*, 1, *19*, 31, 48
English, Frank 171

fairs 29, 38, 71
Fairs, Geoffrey 31, 35, 58, 64
ferry 29, 31, 47
Firefly (fire engine) 119, *120*
fishing 29, 47, 74, 118, 121, 124, 161
FitzOsbern, William 1–6, 15–6, 43
Flanders 3
flannel 29–30, 47, 49, 129
France 22–3, 101, 103–5, 141
Freemasons 98
fulling *see flannel*

Gelli Gandryll, Y 8
Gerald of Wales 10, 16–7
Glasbury *x*, 5, 7, 10–1, 26, 56, 60, 123, 156

Gloucester 15, 16, 114
Glyndŵr, Owain 28, 31–2
Golden Valley *x*, 5, 82, 96
Golesworthy family 82
  Anna (née Valk) viii, 142, 170, 177
  Arthur 142, 175
  Caroline 82, 177–8
  Frank Woodland 82, 141
  Jeanette 177–8
  Robert 83, 160
  Roger 141–2, 160, 170, 177
Griffiths, Charles (land agent) 79, *79*, 93
Griffiths, Robert (solicitor) 93, 107
Griffiths, R. Trevor (solicitor) 65
Gruffydd ap Llewelyn 10
Gwernyfed 138, 140
Gwynn, Elizabeth 43, 64
Gwynn, Howell of Trecastle 38, 41–3

Haddon Bros of Hereford (architects) 75, 81
Hall, Spencer 155–6, 166–7
Harding, Rhys 99, 102, 104, 117
Hardwicke 96
Hay and Brecon Farmers Co-operative 160
Hay Common 130
Hay Gas and Coke Company 63, 135
Hay-on-Wye
  bakers 125, 148–150
  bridges 47–9, *55*, 56, 61, 67–70, *68*, *69*, 101, 127, 133, 153, 157–8
  buildings and businesses (excl. pubs)
    1 Belmont Road *81*, *82*, 108
    1 Garibaldi Terrace 105, 127
    2 St Mary's Villas 104, 130
    3 Broad Street *vi*, *34*, 121, *122*, 139, 150–4, *151*
    6 Broad Street *see also Café Royal* *vi*, 76, 77, 85, 87, *89*, 91–3, 177
    8 Broad Street *vi*, 77, *95*, 153
    9 Broad Street (now 9b) *vi*, 77
    12 Broad Street *vi*, *82*, 85
    13 Broad Street *see also Tinto House* *vi*, *82*

14 Broad Street *vi*, 81, **81**, 82, **82**, 95, 176–7
15 Broad Street *vi*, **82**
20 Broad Street see also Chancery House/ Prospect House *vi*
21 Bear Street *vi*, 120
21 Broad Street see also Montpelier House *vi*, 53
22 Broad Street *vi*, vii, 53, 161, 177
23 Broad Street see also West House *vi*
24 Broad Street see also Sycamore House *vi*
25 Broad Street see also Brynhyfryd *vi*
25a Broad Street *vi*, **52**, 53, 85, 133
28 Broad Street *vi*, 149
30–33 Broad Street see also Tanners Arms *vi*
40 Chancery Lane 75
Agricultural Hall, Lion Street (now the Richard Booth Bookshop) 104, 171, 174, 176
Alan Powell's carpentry workshop *vi*, **121**, 176–7
bakehouse 9, 11
Bank House (now South Bank House) 39, 53, 57–8
Barclays Bank *vi*, 53, 128
Belle Vue *vi*, 79, **79**, **82**, 93, 98, 123, 174
Boardroom, The (now Health Matters) *vi*, 39, 57, **57**, 65, 150
bookshops 33, 159, 161, 165, 171, 173–4, 177,
  Addyman Books 174
  Boz Books (Ty Tan Art gallery) 161
  Broad Street Book Centre see also 6 Broad Street and Café Royal 177
  Cinema Bookshop **171**, 174
  Poetry Bookshop, The 177
  Richard Booth Bookshop, The see also Agricultural Hall 104, 171, 174
  Rose's Children's Bookshop 177
brewery 9, 12
Brynhyfryd *vi*, **52**, 53
Café Royal *vi*, 91–6, **94**, 112, 123, 125–6, 139, **145**, 146–8, 164, 168–70, **169**, 176–7,

bakery 96, 125, 137, 148–50, 169
XL Stores 94–5, **94**, 126, 137, 140, **145**, 146
Castle vii, 1, 4–6, 9–11, 14–5, 18–9, **20**, 22, 24–5, 31, 36, 38, 41–3, **41**, **42**, **46**, 47–8, 72–3, 89, 161–2, 165, **172**, 174, 176, 179
Chancery House see also Prospect House *vi*, 51, 179
Cheese Market 40, **40**,
clock tower *vi*, vii, viii, 50, 53, 63, 78, 80–1, **80**, **82**, **90**, 99, **100**, 110, 119, 143, 146, 151, 164
Crown Hotel *vi*, 74–8, **77**, 81, 102, 118–21, 143–4, 149, 151, 170, 173, 179
Drill Hall 26, 78, 98, 105, 117–8
Ebeneezer Congregational Chapel (The Globe) *vi*, **13**, **49**, 73, 79, **90**, 139, 176
fish shop (Lion Street) 95, 170,
fish and chip shop (Tanners Arms) 139
fish and chip shop (old Post Office) 150, 170
Frank Lewis House 174
Gabb & Co *vi*, 58, 65, 108
Garibaldi Terrace 105, 127, 154
Gas Works, The 63, **64**, 135–8, **135**, 159–60
Globe, The see Ebeneezer Chapel
Golesworthy's *vi*, 82–3, **82**, **83**, 85
Granary, The *vi*, viii, 47, **82**, 175, 177–8
Gypsy Castle Farm 126
Hay Deli 96
Hay Takeaway 150, 170
Keylock's butchers 165, 174
Jones Home Hardware 26, 62, 122, **123**
Limited, The see Agricultural Hall
livery stables 74, 121, 144
London House **82**, 85, **97**, 99, **100**
market hall 40–1
Montpelier House see 21 Broad Street
motte and bailey 5–7, **6**, 35, **61**, 62

INDEX   **193**

Hay-on-Wye buildings and businesses cont.
   Old Electric Shop *see also Crown Hotel* 74, 144
   Old House *see Three Tuns*
   Poplar House *vi*, *13*, 49, 87, 93
   Post Office (Broad Street) *vi*, *86*, 87, 91, 94, 146, 150, 170
   Prospect House (Chancery House) *vi*, 51, 53, *89*, 100, 161–5, *162*, 175, 179
   Rock House *134*, 135, 138
   St John's (church) 15, 19, 43–5, *44*, 51, 73, 153
   St Mary's Church viii, 8, 35, 79, 93, 96, 155
   Salem Baptist Chapel 73, 105
   school 43, 45, 51, 73, 86–7, 91, 126, 132–3, 139, 165
   Swan Hotel *see also Swan Inn* 8, 66, 150
   Sycamore House *vi*, 53
   Tinto House *vi*, 39, 81, *81*, *82*, 108, 113
   town wall 11, 25–6, *26*, 34–5, 48, 154
   Tredegar House *see also pubs/ King's Head vi*, 50
   Webb's garage 120–1, 156–7, 176–7
   West House *vi*, vii, 39, 45, *45*, 53, *89*, 91, 132, 135, 147
   Wigington Antiques 161–3, 176
   Williams Beales & Co. *vi*, 75
   XL Stores *see Café Royal*
burgages 10–2, 14, 16, 19, *19*, 24, 26–9, 36, 74, 126, 151
butchers *vi*, 9, 14, *95*, 153–4, 165, 168, 174
Cats Park 137
cattle market vii, 4–5, 9, 62, 84, 146, 148
chemists 81, 102, 108–9, *109*
grocers 85, *95*, 100, *100*, 102, 125, 126, 170
mill pond 12, 34–5, *90*
mills (Hay water mills) vii, 12–3, *13*, 29–30, 47, 129–30, *130*, 155
millstream 12–3, *13*, 129–32, *131*

pubs 50, 119
   Black Swan *vi*, 39, 43–5, *44*, 48, 50, *89*, *120*, 139, 147, *169*, 170
   Bridge End Inn 119
   Cock Inn (Wye Hotel/ Jones Home Hardware) *61*, 62, 122
   King's Head 50, *50*, 63, *82*
   Lamb Inn 102, 106
   Masons Arms (now SPAR) *171*, 173
   Nelson Inn (Kingfisher House) 70, 119
   Old White Lion 50, *82*, 83, *97*, 119
   Rose and Crown *vi*, 39, 50, 63, 70, 73–8, *77*, 90, 119
   Seven Stars *vi*, *vii*, 39, 50, *82*, 119, 133, 150, 164–5, *164*,
   Ship Inn 119
   Spreadeagle *see Three Tuns*
   Swan Inn 58, *61*, 65–6, 74, 119
   Tanners Arms *vi*, *13*, 119, 139, 149
   Three Tuns *vi*, *34*, 35, 39, 48, 50, *89*, 118–9, 133–4, 139, 150, 156, 179–80, *180*
   Wheatsheaf (now Tomatito's) 51
   Wye Hotel, The (Jones Home Hardware) 62, 122–6, 146
reservoirs (on Hay Common) 130
streets
   Bear Street 18, 24, 28, *42*, 120
   Bell Bank *42*, 73, 105
   Belmont Road *vi*, 6, 24–6, 28, *42*, 43, 78, *81*, *82*, *90*, 98, 108, 122, 143
   Booth Gardens 26, *26*, 154
   Brecon Road *61*, 91, 124, 136
   Bredwardine Road *x*, 5, *19*, 138
   Bridge Street *vi*, 35, *42*, 48, 53, 61, *61*, 67, 70, *89*, *90*, 91–2, 119, 127, *127*, 139, 158, 159
   Brook Street 47, *42*, *90*, 165, 179
   Castle Street 40, 47, 91, 123, 125, 150, 161, 165, 171, 173
   Chancery Lane *also Pig Lane or Gravel Lane vi*, *42*, 47, 51, *51*, 53, 57–8, 65, 75, *90*, 110, 133, 163, 174–5
   Church Street *42*, 120, 170,

Cranbourne Alley *see the Pavement*
Coal Market, The 63, 78, **82**
Gravel Lane *see Chancery Lane*
Heol y Dwr *vi*, 13, 18–9, 24, 28–9, **42**, **49**, 73, 85–6, **90**, 110–2, ***111***, 129, 132–3, 154, 165
Lion Street *vi*, 26, 40, **42**, 78–9, 82–3, ***82***, ***83***, **90**, 104, 117, 120–1, 141, 143, 149–50, 152, 157, 170, 174, 177
Mill Bank housing estate *vi*, 155
Newport Street (Ship Pitch, Watergate Street) 6, 12–3, 25, 34, 43, 50, 63, 70, **90**, 106, 119, ***134***, 135, ***135***
Oxford Road 42, **42**, 47, 144, 165, 174
Pavement, the *vi*, **42**, 50, 63, 78–9, **80**, **82**, 87, **90**, 91, 96, 99, 101, 108, ***109***, 119, 128, 141, 177
Pig Lane *see Chancery Lane*
Potter's Lane (Nantyglasdwr Lane) 139
St John's place **42**, 153, 164
St Mary's Villas 104, 130
Ship Pitch *see Newport Street*
Tump, The 50, 78–9, **80**, **82**, **84**
Watergate Street (Newport St) 34, 43
tannery 12–4, **13**, 30, 49, 129, 155
tramway *see railways*
Hay Urban District Council 129, 167, 174–5
haye 3–5
Haye, La 1–4, 7–9, 11, 24, 43
Henry Somerset (1st duke of Beaufort) 42–3
Hereford 16, 28, 47, 65, 104, 109–10, 134, 150, 159, 178
  Assize Court 112–3, ***114***
Hereford, earl of 1, 4, 15
Hereford Times 56, 67, 71, 117
Herefordshire *x*, 1, 9, 11, 19, 31, 41, 58, 92, 133
Hincks, Dr T.E. (Tom) 81–2, 92, 108–10, 112–4, 116
Hitchcox family 93–6, 104, 122, 124–5, ***124***, 137, 144, 148
  Elizabeth 104

Eric 96, ***124***, ***145***, 168–9, 177
Fanny 104
Frank Edward 93–6, ***93***, 112, 122–4, 144
Jennifer 96, ***124***
Nancy 122, ***124***
Neil 94, 141, 143, 149–50, 153, 163, 168–9
Ruth Francis 96, ***124***
Sarah Ann (née Lane) 92–6, 104, 122–4, ***124***, 137, 139, 141, 144–5
Sylvia 96
Taddy *see Vale*
Hope, George 74
hunting 3, 15, 121

Jenkins, Kelvyn ***171***, 171
John, Maurice (stationmaster) 159
Jones family 99, ***99***, 105, 127–8
  Bernard 99, ***101***, 101–2, 105, 117, 127, 130, 143
  Geoffrey 105, 127–8
  Ken 101, 105, 128, 154
  Ralph 105, 128
  Spencer 99
  Stephen Meredith (tailor) 99, ***97***, 104–5, 127, 142
Jones, Betty *see Breeze family*
Jones, David (accountant) 139
Jones, Martin 139

Kedward, Caleb (grocer) 95, ***95***, 153
Keylock family 143, 155, 165, 174
Kilvert, Revd Francis 71–3, 79, 117
Kings of England
  Edward III 29
  Charles II 42
  Henry I 10–1, 15
  Henry II 16–8
  Henry III 23–5
  Henry VII 40
  Henry VIII 31–3, 37–8
  John 18, 22–4
  Richard I (the Lionheart) 18
  William Rufus 4, 15
  William the Conqueror 4
Kington 4, 61

Lane, Sarah Ann *see Hitchcox*
leather vii, 13–4, 129, 155
Leighton, Jo 175
Leland, John 32–9, 42, 47, 161
Lewis, Elsie 104–5, 127
Lewis, Harry (butcher) 153
Lewis, Nellie (butcher) 153–4, 168
Lilwall, William 86, 96
Llanigon 60, 138
Llewelyn ap Gruffydd (the Last) 36
Llewelyn the Great 22, 24, 36

Magna Carta 22–3
manorial court 9
Marcher lords 2, 4–5, 10–11, 15–7, 31, 37
markets vii, 1, 4–6, 9, 14, 18, 29, 35, 38, 40–1, 43, 48–51, 53, 62–3, 70, 75, 78, **84**, 122, 140, 146–8, 164, 179
  Cobbled pavement market 147, 164
Marshal, Eva *see de Braose*
Marshal, William 23–5
Martin, Oswald (solicitor) 107–8, 110, 113
Matilda, Empress 15
Mavrojani, Capt. 103
Miles of Gloucester 11, 14
milk 96, 102, 126, 139
Moor, The 138, 140–1
Morelli, Leon 51, 179
Morgan, Ellis 168
Morgan, Reg 136–7
Morgan, Sir Charles 60, 66
motte and bailey castles 2, 5–6, **6**

Nest *see Agnest*
de Neufmarché family 11
  Agnest *see Agnest*
  Bernard (Newmarch) 4–5, 9, 11, 14
  Mahel 10–11
  Sybil 10–11, 14–6
Nonconformists (dissenters) 72
Normans 1–22

pigs 12, 51, 153–4
Pitt, Henry 83
Potter, Bill and Florrie 139–40

Powell, Alan (carpenter) 121, 176
Powell, Albert ix, 118–9, 133, 156, 179–80, **180**
Powell, Leslie 118, 179
Powell, Lucy 118, 179–80, **180**
Presteigne 4
Price, DWOP 128
Price, Geoff and Amy 147, 170
Pugh family 91
Pugh, Eric 136
Pugh, John 95
Pugh, Raymond (postman) 167–8
Pugh, Tony ix, 128, 132–3, 143–4, 149, 156, 160, 180
Pugh, William (Billie, or Bill) 91, 95–6, 128, 136, 164

Radnorshire 31, 41, 48, 73, 80, 102
railways 80, **90**
  Golden Valley Railway 78
  Hay Railway (tramway) 58–66, **61**, **62**, 70, 78, 136
  Hereford, Hay and Brecon Railway, The 25–6, 56, 66–71, **69**, 85, **90**, 95–6, 123, 125, 129–30, **135**, 138, 159–61, **160**
  Kington Railway 61
Ratcliffe, Dai 148–50, 169–70
Revolt of the Earls 4
River Wye *see brooks and rivers*
Roger, earl of Hereford (son of Miles of Gloucester) 15
Romans 3, 36

Savin, Thomas (contractor) 66–70, **68**, **69**, 74–5, 78, 153, 158
Scotland Yard detectives 110, 151
Sinclair, Julie (née Julysia Webb) 132, 141, 151, 153, 157
slaughterhouses 14, 153–4, 158, 168
Somerset, Henry, 1st duke of Beaufort 42
Spencer, James (solicitor) 57–60, 63–5, 79, 174
Spilsbury, Sir Bernard 113, 121
Stevenson, Anne 177
Stokoe family 51

Freddy 117–8
Thomas (Tom) (Councillor) 100, 102–3, 106, 117

tailoring 99, 104–5, 127–8, 142
Talgarth 59–60, 133, 141, 156
Terrett, William (grocer) 84, 100
Tewdwr, Rhys ap 4–5
Thomas, Daisy 72–3
Thornton, Pat 162–3, 165, 175–6, **176**
trains *see railways*
Turnpike Trusts 48–9, 59, 79

Vale, Mr (saddler) 14, 155, 157
Vale, Taddy (née Hitchcox) 104, 155

Wallis, Thomas (grocer and postmaster) 85–7, **86**, 91, 93
Walwyn (family name) 28, 36
war
  black market 141
  civil war of 1139–53 15–6
  First World War 98–105, 107, 126, 134, 169
    Mametz Wood, Battle of 103, 105, 127
    R.A.M.C. (Royal Army Medical Corps) 102, 104
    South Wales Borderers, The 101
    volunteer force 78, 98, 102–3
    Ypres, Battle of 105
    munitions (Rotherwas) 104, 138
  Second World War 105, 137–44, 180
    American soldiers 138–9, 141, 150, 180
    evacuees 138–9, 147
    Home Guard (Local Defence Volunteers) 105
    VE Day 143–4
    Territorial Armies 100–1, 105
    Tribunal 96, 103
Warren, the **42**, **61**, 118
water supply 130, 155
Watkins, Potty (baker) 149–50
Webb family 119–21, **122**, 139, 150–4, 156–7, 176–7
  Frank 119–20
  Humphrey 121, 139, 149–51, 157, 176–7
  Humphrey Vines (HV) 119–22, 139, 151–2
  Irene 149, 151–2, **151**, 154
  James 119–20
  Julysia *see Julie Sinclair*
wells 8
  Eye Well 8
  St Mary's Well 8
  Swan Well 8, **8**, 130
  Walk Well 8
Welsh border 1, 119
Westbrook Farm 96, 122, 126, 145
Whitney-on-Wye 43, 56, 92
Wigington family 51, 161–2, 165, 175–6, 179
  Bryan 161–3, 165, 175
  Colin 161–3
  Pat *see Thornton*
Wilding, Valerie 144, 146
Wilson, Mr (dentist) and Mrs 132–4, 180
de Winton, Revd J.J. 93, 96, 98–9, 102, 114